PRAISE FOR

Why Flying Is Miserable

"With careful research and clear thinking, Sitaraman outlines a plan to ensure that the airline business works for everyone."
Kirkus Reviews

"With characteristic intelligence and eloquence, Ganesh Sitaraman has given us a compelling case for reforming a key element of our economic and cultural lives: the air industry. This is a policy argument that can make a difference. Highly recommended!"
JON MEACHAM,
Pulitzer Prize—winning author and historian

"Whether it's the unreliable service, the massive bailouts or the combination of high prices and bad service, the airline industry has come to encapsulate all that has gone wrong in late-stage American capitalism. This book makes it clear we need to rethink how we manage the essential industries in our time and ultimately delivers an inspiring message: this is our country, and we can do better."
TIM WU,
author of *The Curse of Bigness*, former special assistant to President Biden for technology and competition policy

"With vivid examples and deft historical analysis, Sitaraman presents a surprisingly gripping account of the structural challenges behind the often-miserable modern experience of flying. His creative and compelling proposals for reclaiming public control over airlines provide an important vision for the future of aviation in this country."
SHELLEY WELTON,
University of Pennsylvania Carey Law School

Why Flying Is Miserable
And How to Fix It

COLUMBIA GLOBAL REPORTS
NEW YORK

Why Flying Is Miserable
And How to Fix It

Ganesh Sitaraman

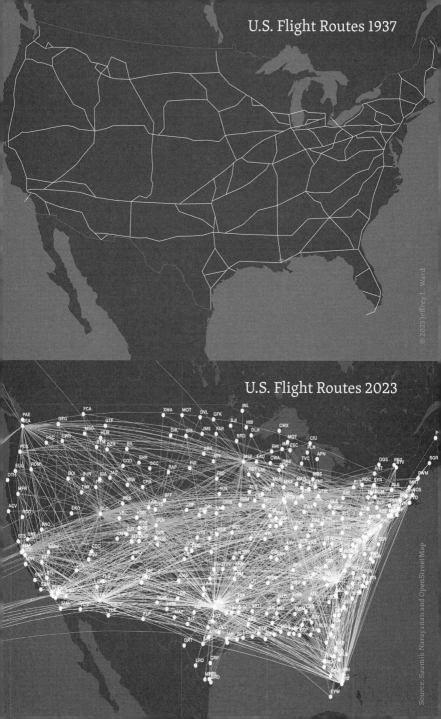

U.S. Flight Routes 1937

U.S. Flight Routes 2023

Why Flying Is Miserable
And How to Fix It
Copyright © 2023 by Ganesh Sitaraman

Published by Columbia Global Reports
91 Claremont Avenue, Suite 515
New York, NY 10027
globalreports.columbia.edu
facebook.com/columbiaglobalreports
@columbiaGR

Library of Congress Cataloging-in-Publication Data

Names: Sitaraman, Ganesh, author.
Title: Why flying is miserable : and how to fix it / Ganesh Sitaraman.
Description: New York, NY : Columbia Global Reports, 2023. | Includes
    bibliographical references.
Identifiers: LCCN 2023011783 (print) | LCCN 2023011784 (ebook) |
    ISBN 9798987053584 (paperback) | ISBN 9798987053591 (ebook)
Subjects: LCSH: Airlines—United States. | Airlines—Government
    policy—United States. | Airlines—United States—Finance.
Classification: LCC HE9803.A4 S58 2023 (print) | LCC HE9803.A4 (ebook) |
    DDC 387.7/0973—dc23/eng/20230505
LC record available at https://lccn.loc.gov/2023011783
LC ebook record available at https://lccn.loc.gov/2023011784

Book design by Strick&Williams
Map design by Jeffrey L. Ward
Author photograph by Sandy Campbell

Printed in the United States of America

CONTENTS

Introduction

Flying is a miracle. For most of human history, it seemed like an impossible dream. But today we take for granted that we can have breakfast in Chicago and dinner in Los Angeles, or see family across the country during Thanksgiving. We can conduct business anywhere. We can visit all the wonders of the world.

But flying is also miserable. Tens of thousands of flights are delayed and canceled each year. As a result, we've missed weddings, had our vacations shortened, lost time with friends, and skipped important meetings. When flights are on time, we pay extra to check our bags and then worry that they'll get lost. The overhead bin space seems to shrink every year—just like the amount of leg room. Delays might mean hours sitting on the tarmac, wishing for a drink of water or a snack or a chance to run to the bathroom. Or they can mean missing a tight connection and being stranded in an unfamiliar city. For those in cities with small airports or airports dominated by one big airline, minimal competition means higher ticket prices. For others, flying is a challenge because the airlines don't serve their city at all. And all of us struggle to navigate the dizzying array of airline statuses and hierarchies, credit card perks, and point systems.

And that's just the passenger experience. Zooming out, the airline industry faces a great deal of, well, turbulence. That turbulence has huge impacts on the country, cities, workers, and the economy. Consider these dynamics:

- Airlines have gone bankrupt over and over again—and in recent years, merged over and over again. There are now only four big US carriers (Delta, American, United, and Southwest).
- In the years before the COVID-19 pandemic, the airlines made record profits. But when the pandemic hit in 2020, they needed huge public support programs—their second in twenty years.
- In 2022 alone, more than 180,000 flights were canceled. Some were because of the Southwest Airlines debacle during the December holidays. But many others were a function of staff shortages or extreme weather at major hub airports.
- Pilots, flight attendants, and other airline employees are often overworked to the point of exhaustion. Meanwhile, unruly travelers are an increasing problem.
- Airlines are now reducing service from midsized cities, like Toledo, Ohio, and Dubuque, Iowa. In some markets like Cheyenne, the state capital of Wyoming, city leaders have even agreed to pay the airlines to offer service because,

despite making profits, airlines refuse to fly there without a revenue guarantee.

The miseries of flying and the turbulence in the industry aren't inevitable—and they aren't just the result of the pandemic. Nor is this a simple story of corporate mismanagement. As varied as these problems are, they stem from a single source: public policy. We make choices as a country—through our elected representatives—about how best to govern our economy. We choose to have rules to ensure that food doesn't have bacteria in it, that our rivers and lakes aren't polluted, that toasters and cars and children's toys are safe. We choose to have a whole set of laws so banks can get chartered, offer loans, and hold our money safely with a federal insurance system in case the bank goes under. We choose to have electricity networks that bring power and light to the country, and we choose to have rules to make sure electricity is affordable so everyone can get service. In all these areas, and more, we have historically chosen a regime of regulated capitalism that has enabled a thriving economy, but one with guardrails to make sure that the dynamics of the market don't lead to destructive harms. Businesses are supposed to follow the rules we set, and be held accountable when they violate the rules. The key question for air travel—or anything else—is simple: What rules should we choose?

Since the Wright Brothers first took flight at Kitty Hawk, North Carolina, in 1903, the United States has tried three different approaches for governing air travel. During the infancy of flight, the federal government promoted the creation and growth

of airlines, largely through subsidies. Once airlines were established, fierce competition led to industry chaos. Congress then
adopted the second approach. It took a page from the American
tradition of regulated capitalism and brought airlines under
a system of governance akin to other transportation industries. The American tradition of regulated capitalism was built
on the understanding that some sectors of the economy were
not like others. Sectors like transportation, communications,
energy, and banking were often networklike; they had tendencies to become monopolies or oligopolies; and they could place
extraordinary power in the hands of a small number of people
and firms. Because of these dynamics, unrestricted competition
wouldn't work in those areas: it would lead to chaos or concentration. One solution is to nationalize businesses in these sectors. Indeed, some countries have had nationalized or publicly
run airlines, trains, telephone systems, and electricity utilities.
But the American way was different. Instead of nationalization,
these sectors were regulated as public utilities. Public utilities
are essential infrastructure—critical for commerce, social life,
and national security. Reliability and stability are paramount.
From 1938 to 1978, air travel was governed under this regime.
The American tradition offered a system of *structural regulations* that together achieved a variety of national goals. The system was designed to serve small and mid-sized communities;
to prevent airline bankruptcies and bailouts; to ensure airports
wouldn't be dominated by one airline; to avoid monopolization and predation; and to maintain stable, reliable service at all
times. It did this through a set of rules that included the regulation of prices, routes, and entry into the airline business. During

14   this period a relatively small number of highly regulated big air-
      lines dominated the market. The legal system ensured that the
      airlines offered high-quality service throughout the country—
      and prevented the abuses that naturally come with limited com-
      petition. It was an age of regulated oligopoly.

         In the 1970s, this system came under pressure from left and
      right, leading to the Airline Deregulation Act of 1978 and a third
      approach to governance. Advocates for deregulation thought
      air travel was not a special sector, akin to a public utility. They
      saw airlines as an ordinary market service, like selling sofas or
      running a convenience store, and they wanted to let the mar-
      ketplace work. By eliminating structural regulation, anyone
      with resources could start an airline (or so they said), and air-
      lines could pick their routes and set their own prices. Increased
      competition would lead to cheaper flights. Advocates didn't
      think that deregulation would have negative effects on small
      or mid-sized communities or that it would lead to concentra-
      tion into a tiny number of dominant airlines. They even claimed
      that after deregulation there could be up to 200 airlines oper-
      ating efficiently. At first, the deregulators looked as if they had
      been right. Opening up competition led immediately to a rush
      of new entrants, lower prices, and fare wars in the early 1980s.
      But by the end of the decade, the airline industry was in cri-
      sis: bankruptcies, low profits, higher prices in some markets,
      labor-management conflicts, a worsening flight experience,
      increased congestion. Leading advocates admitted that they had
      misunderstood that airline markets are monopolistic or oli-
      gopolistic, that they didn't realize how important scale was to
      the airline business, and that they didn't foresee many of these
      ill-effects. Some politicians even apologized for deregulation.

And the four biggest airlines ultimately ended up with an even larger share of the market than before—but now without the duties or restraints of the regulated era. Airlines had become an *unregulated* oligopoly.

We have now lived under this system for more than forty years. In that time, there have been 189 bankruptcy filings in the industry, major carriers have shifted pension obligations to the government, the number of major airlines has shrunk, and the government has had to bail out the industry. Fees are higher, seats are smaller, and the experience of flying seems to be getting worse.

Then came the pandemic. The COVID-19 pandemic revealed for everyone how problematic our system of unregulated oligopoly is. Before the pandemic, the big airlines were flush with cash. So much so that American Airlines' CEO Doug Parker predicted they would never lose money ever again. American alone issued stock buybacks amounting to $12.9 billion between 2013 and 2019—more than its annual payroll in a given year. But when the pandemic hit, air travel grounded to a halt. By April of 2020, passenger travel was down 96 percent compared to one year earlier. Without much of a rainy-day fund, the once-flush airlines asked Congress for funding to cover their payroll in the spring of 2020. Some commentators observed that airlines didn't need this support. They had highly valuable frequent flyer programs they could use as collateral to get private sector loans. If private sector funding was insufficient, they could file for bankruptcy, as they had in the past. Doing so would not liquidate the company or significantly disrupt air travel. Congress rejected these arguments, given the airlines' status as an essential part of our commercial infrastructure.

16   The CARES Act of 2020 was a critically important piece of legislation, designed to prevent the catastrophic collapse of the airline industry—and in particular, to save the wages and jobs of workers—by authorizing $50 billion in loans and grants. Under the payroll support program, airlines were offered up to $25 billion to cover their employee salaries and benefits without layoffs. This program was extended twice, with total authorized spending ultimately running to $54 billion. American took $12.74 billion, Delta $11.88 billion, United $10.89 billion, Southwest $7.1 billion. The program was transparent, protected workers, and prevented the airlines from profiting off of taxpayer funds. Airlines couldn't fire or involuntarily furlough employees until September 30, 2021, couldn't issue stock buybacks or dividends, and couldn't increase executive compensation.

But in a quest to cut costs, airlines offered early retirement and voluntary furloughs, leave, and reduced hours to employees. Thousands of employees took up these offers, which included cash severance packages and generous benefits. While technically legal, early retirements certainly violated the spirit of the law. The point of the payroll support program and its no-layoffs condition was to allow the airlines to weather the downturn. When travel perked back up, they would be ready to fly without delays or disruptions.

But when passengers did start traveling again, the airlines had too few staff. They canceled flights by the thousands. There were almost twice as many cancellations in 2022, as compared to the average over the prior decade. Airlines also pushed pilots, flight attendants, and ground crews harder. Pilots for some airlines were flying six days a week, and fatigue rates were 350 percent higher than before the pandemic. Airlines argued that the problem was too few pilots, due to minimum flight training requirements. Proposals emerged to lower training standards and increase the retirement age to allow older pilots to keep flying. But these proposals overlooked both the most immediate problem—the early retirement packages—and the deeper ones—pay and training pipelines. As the pilots' union observed, some airlines had more pilots than before COVID, but were flying fewer routes and having a hard time recruiting pilots for low pay. And unlike foreign airlines, the biggest US carriers only started pilot training programs in the last few years.

With tens of thousands of flight cancellations and with workforce shortages, the airlines started cutting back on routes, in some cases ending service to entire cities. In the fall of 2022, American cut 28,000 flights—17 percent of its flights in November. This included hundreds of flights from large cities like Pittsburgh, Pennsylvania. Smaller cities are seeing airlines depart altogether. Since the pandemic, American, Delta, and United have dropped fifty-nine cities from service. American has abandoned New Haven, Connecticut; Duluth, Minnesota; and Ithaca, New York. Delta has left Santa Barbara, California; Flint, Michigan; and Lincoln, Nebraska. United no longer serves Flagstaff, Arizona; Tallahassee, Florida; or Pierre, South Dakota. For some cities, the departure of its only airline means no daily flight service whatsoever. In September 2022, Toledo, Ohio, a city of about 270,000 with a metro area of 600,000 people, lost daily flight service when American ended its last remaining route. In the 1970s, Toledo had service from five carriers, and United alone offered eleven daily flights to seven different cities.

18   As an individual passenger, these post-pandemic challenges are frustrating. But for the country, a broken airline system is a crisis. Air travel is a basic piece of infrastructure for
society—like roads, electricity, or the internet. Think about it
this way. Imagine if you live in a city that has lost almost all service, like Dubuque, Iowa.* It's now much harder for friends and
family to visit. Fewer tourists will see the National Mississippi
River Museum or the Dubuque Arboretum. It'll be difficult for
businesspeople to come to town for a sales call or a convention.
And it's hard to imagine a local entrepreneur with an innovative
idea staying in Dubuque to build the next Fortune 500 company.
Recruits might not want to move to a place where it would be
extremely hard to fly home. Vendors and clients will have a challenging time traveling to headquarters for meetings. And the
entrepreneur will spend hundreds of valuable hours on the road,
rather than building the business. If people and regions everywhere in the country are going to have the opportunity to succeed, they need access to flights. Whether for pleasure, tourism,
or commerce, air travel is critical infrastructure in the modern
world.

      With the pandemic in the rearview mirror, the verdict is in.
American air travel is getting worse. We now have fewer flights
to fewer places with less competition and higher prices—and
with overworked pilots, flight attendants, and employees. The
CARES Act succeeded in preventing the worst-case scenario:
bankruptcies, further consolidation, mass layoffs, and the

* A few months after losing service from American Airlines, a small carrier
called Avelo Airlines announced it would start twice-weekly flights from
Dubuque to Orlando.

hobbling of the industry. But it was not designed to address the underlying problems with flying—problems that were getting worse well before the pandemic.

The time has come to take a fresh look at what's gone wrong in air travel and how we can make it better. We now have sufficient experience with deregulation—and distance from the turn away from structural regulation—to reflect more carefully on both approaches, assess their benefits and drawbacks, and consider new directions for the governance of air travel.

More broadly, in recent years, scholars, commentators, and policymakers on the left and right have been reevaluating the neoliberal economic ideology that dominated from the 1970s to the 2010s. Things that had been unimaginable over the last generation now command cross-partisan support. On both right and left, antitrust enforcement is resurgent. Congress has passed major bipartisan industrial policy legislation—investing billions of dollars in making things in America and reshoring supply chains. Presidents Trump and Biden have both taken a less globalizing approach to international trade policy. And leaders in both parties have been more open to new thinking on taxes, spending, and deficits. In the midst of these big changes, remembering and reviving the American tradition of regulated capitalism should be on the table too.

To get behind the daily headlines and truly understand the miseries of flying, we have to uncover the hidden incentives that shape air travel. And that means digging into the structure and economic dynamics of the industry and the history of airline regulation. Chapter 1 takes us back to the early days of flight and describes how the federal government subsidized the creation of the airline industry in the early twentieth century and then provided a regulatory framework starting in 1938 to ensure stable, reliable air service all across the country. Chapter 2 tackles the marquee event in the history of airlines: the deregulation of the industry in 1978. It recounts why advocates wanted to deregulate the industry, what they predicted would happen, and how they implemented deregulation after they were successful. In chapter 3, we turn to the great debate over airlines since 1978: Was deregulation successful? Looking at the ten years after deregulation, we will see that the advocates were mostly proven wrong in their predictions—and some eventually admitted it. Chapter 4 tells the story of airlines in the age of deregulation, including the booms, the busts, and the bailouts of the last thirty years. What this history shows is that the problems with flying today are a function of the economic dynamics of the industry—dynamics that the American tradition of regulated capitalism tamed and that deregulation unleashed.

Finally, in chapter 5, we turn to the solutions. We need to start by recognizing that airlines are more like public utilities than ordinary consumer products, and we need to keep in mind the many goals of an airline system: stable and resilient service, national security, geographic access, passenger experience, and consumer prices. Taking both the dynamics of the industry and the goals of a national airline policy into account yields three principles for reform: (1) No more flyover country. There should be access to air travel all across the United States. (2) No bailouts, no bankruptcies. We want an industry that is stable, reliable, innovative, and thriving. (3) Fair and transparent prices. We should make sure consumers everywhere can afford to travel and know what they're getting. If we can get these big pieces right—if we get the structure for governing air travel right—a lot of the daily irritations and frustrations will go away on their own.

There are many ways to achieve these goals. We could nationalize the airlines, as some have suggested. We could have one airline operate as a regulated monopoly. We could establish a "public option" for air travel. Or we could preserve competition but under a system of regulation. Whichever approach one favors, the most important lesson is this: in a democracy, we the people get to choose how we live and how our industries are governed. And we can choose to have an airline industry that reaches more places, at fair prices, and with a higher quality of service. We can choose to fix flying.

The Rise of Airline Regulation

To understand the dynamics that make flying miserable today, we have to start with history. Airlines currently operate within a legal structure that was established in 1978 with the Airline Deregulation Act. Deregulation was a reaction to the regulated system that had governed air travel since 1938. This earlier system had its own logic and goals. Its structural approach drew on hundreds of years of tradition and was distinctly American. Many people don't know how that system worked—and many probably don't realize that the way airlines used to operate was very different than it is today.

By looking at why the structural approach emerged in the 1930s, how it worked, and why and how it was changed, we can understand the dynamics that the Airline Deregulation Act unleashed. This chapter tells that story—and sets the stage for appreciating the turbulence in the airline industry since.

The Newest Avenue of the Sky

From the very beginning, the US government was interested in supporting the development of flight. In the 1890s, the secretary of the Smithsonian, Samuel Langley, developed an unmanned aircraft that he called an "aerodrome." With a successful test flight in 1896, the War Department gave Langley $50,000 to develop a manned aerodrome. Langley produced the aircraft, but it failed spectacularly, crashing into the Potomac River in December 1903. Only a few days later, the Wright brothers made their historic flight at Kitty Hawk, North Carolina. With those twelve seconds, the aerial age began.

For the next few decades, the driving force behind the development and expansion of air travel in the United States was, perhaps surprisingly, the Post Office. Since the founding of the country, the Post Office had tried to ensure that mail delivery would always be as rapid as the fastest mode of communication possible. The Post Office contracted with the Pony Express in the 1860s. It sorted mail on train cars to speed up delivery in the late nineteenth century. And with the invention of the airplane, it wanted to transport mail by air. In 1918, Congress initiated an experimental airmail service, which the Army operated for a few months before the Post Office took over. The Post Office realized quickly that contracting with private airlines would be easier than running an airline itself. And with foreign countries investing in the development of airlines, there was added pressure for the US to keep up. Congress stepped in and passed the Airmail Act of 1925 (also known as the Kelly Act). The Kelly Act provided subsidies for airlines that would carry mail. The hope was that funding from the government would spur capitalists to invest in creating airlines by guaranteeing a return on their investment in the form of contracts to carry mail. Unfortunately, the act was poorly designed and problems emerged almost immediately. As one scholar observed,

24 "Contracts were limited by . . . provisions of law to four-year periods, offering little security for the necessary investment; and the compensation permitted by the act was too limited and uncertain."

Over the next twelve years, federal policy toward airlines was unstable. The Air Commerce Act of 1926 brought some coordination and security to the emerging industry. It required airlines to register aircraft; mandated that planes be flown by certified airmen; and facilitated the creation of air traffic control rules. Two years later, in 1928, Congress passed a statute trying to fix the problems in the Kelly Act by extending airmail contracts to ten years. With a longer term of years and an anticipated increase in the volume of mail transported, airlines would be able to recover the high costs of ground facilities that could not be recouped within the shorter four-year period.

These developments happened during the "roaring '20s," and airlines were part of that era's irrational economic exuberance. With Charles Lindbergh's world-famous flight from New York to Paris in 1927, the industry got caught up in a "speculative boom" in which "[a]lmost any type of airline stock could be sold." A railroad called "Seaboard Air Line" even saw a spike in its stock price, simply because of confusion from its name. Airlines were proliferating quickly, and some were operating at a loss. Meanwhile, postal expenditures were up, due to rising volumes.

The stock market crash in 1929 and the onset of the Great Depression brought an end to this period. Airlines were now in a dire situation. They were losing money rapidly. They were cutting prices to try to spur demand. But they were still under severe economic pressure. A wave of mergers followed. One set

of smaller airlines that combined during this period became
American Airways—later renamed American Airlines.

Faced with a crisis in the airline industry, Herbert Hoover's postmaster general, Walter Brown, wanted to fix the system. He hoped to encourage the use of bigger and more advanced planes, which would improve service, increase passenger traffic, and simultaneously save money for the Post Office. In 1930, Brown pushed Congress to pass the McNary-Watres Act. The act authorized the postmaster general to award airmail contracts to the lowest bidder and to extend or consolidate routes if the postmaster thought doing so was in the public interest. These were expansive powers—enough to restructure the whole industry—and Brown took them up with enthusiasm. He began hosting meetings with the industry to determine how to consolidate routes and merge firms together. Fewer firms would mean less speculation and wasted capital, less competition, and more stability. Brown's "Progressive Republican vision involved an integrated national network of transcontinental lines operated by large, well-financed corporations in regulated competition with one another." When the comptroller of the United States interpreted the law narrowly, Brown found a work-around. Brown's process of route consolidation, coupled with mergers in the industry, led quickly to the creation of major airlines TWA and United. Under Brown's tenure, the fortunes of airlines started to change. Airlines were again growing and making money, and airmail costs for the Post Office were falling—from $1.26 per mile to 26 cents per mile between 1929 and 1933.

When Democrats gained power in 1933, then-senator (and later Supreme Court justice) Hugo Black took aim at Brown's

26   actions. Black decried the anticompetitive system Brown created, and smaller, independent airlines joined in the attack as well. After Black opened hearings and investigations, reporters began to characterize Brown's meetings with industry as corrupt "spoils conferences." For his part, Brown did not to keep his actions secret. While he may have been creative in his legal maneuvers, he believed Congress had authorized him to wield expansive powers, and he even issued press releases announcing his meetings. But when one Hoover administration official refused to testify before Black's committee, Brown's work took on the atmosphere of scandal.

In 1934, the new postmaster general canceled all airmail contracts based on the justification that Brown and the airlines had conspired to prevent competitive bidding. President Franklin Delano Roosevelt then shifted all airmail operations to the Army Air Corps. But the Army Air Corps was ill-suited for the task. Among other things, its pilots had not been trained to fly in inclement weather or at night. In just a few months, sixty-six planes crashed and twelve people were killed.

Roosevelt and the Democratic Congress backtracked immediately amid public outcry. The swiftly passed Airmail Act of 1934 adopted a system of competitive bidding, with initial year-long contracts that could be extended indefinitely. The law gave the Interstate Commerce Commission (ICC)—which regulated other types of transportation, like railroads—the power to review airmail rates. The Airmail Act included antimonopoly provisions that prohibited airlines from becoming conglomerates, creating holding companies, or having overlapping boards of directors or shareholders. It also prevented airlines from leveraging their government-subsidized businesses into power

over other parts of the industry. A firm with an airmail contract
could not hold stock or interest in any firm "engaged directly or
indirectly in any phase of the aviation industry." This provision
forced existing aviation holding companies to divest and separate their various businesses—creating many of the big aviation
companies we know today. United, for example, separated into
United Air Lines and the Boeing Aircraft Company.

The 1934 Airmail Act also tried to exclude from future contracts any individuals and airlines that had been involved in
Brown's so-called spoils conferences. When competitive bidding for airmail routes took place after the 1934 Act, individuals who had met with Postmaster General Brown were thus
unable to participate. But their firms, now reorganized with
minor name changes, were awarded similar routes to those they
had previously flown. "These airlines had the equipment, per-
sonnel, money, and infrastructure already in place along these
routes, as Walter Brown had always asserted. Realistically, no
independent airline stood a chance of flying the mail more efficiently or safely."

The 1934 system, however, also didn't work. For one thing,
regulatory authority was divided. The Commerce Department
regulated safety; the Post Office issued mail contracts; the ICC
reviewed airmail rates. But the dynamics in the industry were
also problematic. Airmail carriers wanted to build out their networks, in part to take advantage of demand from increasing passenger travel. They thought some routes would eventually be
so valuable that airlines began to underbid to win the right to
serve them. In perhaps the most extreme case, Eastern Air Lines
in 1938 "bid zero cents per mile for the right to carry airmail
between Houston and San Antonio."

28   The airline industry itself was deeply concerned. Colonel Edgar Gorrell was president of the newly formed Air Transport Association (ATA), a trade association for the airlines. Gorrell believed that unregulated competition in the sector was destructive. Airlines were not able to raise private capital, in part because fierce competition had meant so many airlines had gone out of business. "A hundred scheduled lines have traversed the airways in a struggle to build this newest avenue of the sky," he told Congress. "But today, scarcely more than a score of those companies remain." With that track record, financiers no longer wanted to waste money on the sector. Meanwhile, in Europe, the rivalry between nations had led to government support and, as a result, a rapidly growing airline system. From Gorrell's perspective, there were only two ways to bring stability and capital investment to the industry:

> One is the way toward which the governments of foreign lands increasingly tend—the way of mounting governmental subsidies, whereby public funds are poured without stint into air transport. The other way is the traditional American way, a way which invites the confidence of the investing public by providing a basic economic charter that promises the hope of stability and security, and orderly and intelligent growth under watchful governmental supervision.

The American Tradition of Regulated Capitalism

When Gorrell invoked "the traditional American way," he didn't mean that airlines should be governed by free markets or *laissez-faire* principles. Rather, Gorrell thought airlines should be regulated under what were then called common carrier or public utility principles, and which some scholars now call the law of networks, platforms, and utilities (NPUs). These principles were critical to what we can think of as the American tradition of regulated capitalism. The American tradition of regulated capitalism had its roots in three different areas of law and policy: communications (the postal system), money (the banking system), and the English law of innkeepers and common carriers, which went all the way back to the thirteenth century. There was no single moment of its founding, no single theorist responsible for its creation, and no manifesto outlining its tenets. It was, truly, a tradition—a set of practices and principles that evolved and was refined over generations.

The central insight was that some sectors of the economy were different than others. Some businesses were critically important to commerce, social life, and national success and security because they had infrastructural features. Under the common law of the Middle Ages and into the nineteenth century, for example, these businesses and professions included markets, mills, inns, ferries, blacksmiths, wharfs, and carriage companies, among many others. With industrialization and new technological developments, scholars, judges, and policymakers alike recognized that grain elevators, slaughterhouses, the telegraph, the telephone, railroads, pipelines, and local utilities like electricity, water, and sewer service also fit into this category.

What makes these areas distinctive? At their core, these are all important services that facilitated a wide range of other commercial and social activities. Without reliable service, critical aspects of commerce and daily life would come to a standstill.

30   But they are also businesses in which there is a tendency toward
       monopoly (single-firm dominance of the market), oligopoly (a
       few firms dominating the market), or "virtual monopoly" (a sit-
       uation in which a business has monopoly-like power over a cus-
       tomer, even though it is not literally a monopoly).

       Consider the telephone. Telephone systems tend toward
       consolidation because of both high capital costs of invest-
       ment and network effects. For telephone companies, it would
       be very expensive—and very crowded—for multiple companies
       to put in telephone poles and lines across the country and to
       every single home. One set of poles and lines would be cheaper
       and better. For users, a telephone network is much more valu-
       able if everyone is on the same network. As a result of these two
       features, it is more efficient for there to be one single system.
       The problem is that a single telephone network would then be a
       monopoly, and with monopoly comes a variety of dangers. The
       company could charge higher prices to users and offer worse
       quality service. It might buy up businesses in downstream sec-
       tors and then use its power in the telephone market to crush its
       downstream competitors. This kind of thing actually happened.
       In one Kentucky lawsuit in the 1880s, for example, a telephone
       company that also owned a carriage business denied phone ser-
       vice to a competitor carriage company. The competitor sued
       because it wanted customers to be able to call and book its ser-
       vices (and it won).

       Some NPUs do not tend toward consolidation because of
       capital costs or network effects, but instead are characterized as
       "virtual" monopolies. Inns are the classic example. In the late
       Middle Ages, a traveler on a road might come to the only inn for
       miles. The traveler might not be able to make it to the next inn

up the road. If the roads are dangerous at night, or if it is cold and raining, the traveler must stay at the inn. But this puts the innkeeper in a dangerously powerful position: the innkeeper could charge exorbitant rates to the traveler. After all, the risk of sleeping outdoors could be theft or even death.

The American tradition recognized the difference between infrastructural enterprises and ordinary businesses from the very start. The US Constitution empowered Congress to create a postal system. The postal system has always had distinctive regulatory features. First and foremost, it was designed to be a single, public system. Rather than featuring competition between private businesses, the Post Office was—and remains—a national monopoly. It is illegal for private companies or individuals to enter the marketplace as competitors for carrying regularly scheduled mail. This single system makes it easy to send mail across the country. It also enables a second feature, which later generations of Americans referred to as the "post office principle." To deliver a letter to a rural area is much more expensive than to send one within a city or between cities. Especially in the early republic, these high costs made it difficult to stitch together people across the vast geography of the United States. To encourage nationwide commerce and civic communication, the postal system set prices using what are called *cross-subsidies*. Rather than set the price of mailing a letter at the cost of delivering it, postage rates are set uniformly—everyone pays the same price today for a stamp, regardless of where the letter is going. This means, in effect, that the price of sending a letter to a rural place is discounted. The early Congresses also set the price of sending newspapers at a discount. While this made urban mail and ordinary

32 correspondence more expensive, the cross-subsidy had the effect of enabling communication and news to far-flung places. The postal monopoly and post office principle were tightly connected. Without a monopoly, private mail carriers would enter the market and carry letters only on the least-expensive, highest-volume, and most-profitable routes. This practice is called *cream-skimming*. If cream-skimming takes hold, rural and distant areas of the country would be left without service, or the government would have to pay exorbitant costs to serve them. Over the course of the nineteenth and twentieth centuries, these regulatory principles enabled the Post Office to provide reliable, universal service—from big cities to the Alaskan bush country—all at an affordable price. In communications, the American tradition would most notably apply to the telephone, which operated as a regulated national monopoly under AT&T for much of the twentieth century.

The American tradition also had roots in money and banking. When Alexander Hamilton proposed the creation of a national bank, he recognized that national provision of the infrastructure of finance would help expand commerce throughout the fledgling republic. When the Second National Bank's charter wasn't renewed during Andrew Jackson's presidency, the country almost immediately fell into a financial panic and depression. In the 1860s, the Lincoln administration established the National Bank Act, which sought to end the "wildcat" era of banking, and instead create a national banking system. Rather than a national monopoly, like the Post Office, the national banking system outsourced the creation of money to private banks—but banks would be chartered and supervised by the federal government. Over time, the banking system included principles of diffusion (restrictions on bank consolidation), "structural separations" (preventing bankers from engaging in other kinds of commercial activity), and rate regulation (both for deposits and between banks).

The American tradition's third source was English law, including the common law. The common law is judge-made law. Judges draw on past cases, tradition, and logic to achieve just outcomes. As early as the thirteenth century, English law and then later, American law, developed a distinctive legal regime to govern networks, platforms, and utilities. This approach generally included three important features. First, during this era, NPU businesses usually were specially chartered by the government, which gave them a legal privilege to run their business—and often precluded competitors from entering the marketplace. These charters ensured that investors would gain a return on their capital investments and it prevented price wars that could destroy multiple competitors at once. Second, NPUs could not exclude customers if they had capacity and the customer was not disruptive. In the words of the common law, they had to "accept all comers" without discrimination. The rule ensured that the monopoly granted by a charter (or that emerged from network effects) would not give the NPU the power to withhold their essential service from some users, or to privilege some users over others. Third, NPUs had to charge just and reasonable rates—that is, fair prices. A duty to serve isn't worth much if the price of service is out of reach. Courts regularly enforced these rules from the Middle Ages through the nineteenth century.

34   In the later nineteenth century, policymakers increasingly placed these rules and requirements into legislation. Concerns about the telegraph and local utilities were widespread, but the marquee effort was to tame the railroads. By the 1860s and 1870s, the railroad industry featured a range of predatory and socially destructive practices. When routes were competitive, rate wars pushed railroads into bankruptcy because they were charging below their costs. Truces came in the form of cartels. Some railroads would build new tracks solely to get bought out by bigger competitors, misusing eminent domain powers. For their part, railroad barons seeking to monopolize the market would threaten to stop connecting with other railroads unless they sold. Rural areas without competition paid exorbitant prices and effectively subsidized competitive markets between cities. And prices were not uniform: large shippers often received special deals that gave them a competitive advantage.

Frustration with these practices led to the creation of state regulatory commissions—expert administrative bodies—that could regulate railroad rates and practices. When the Supreme Court struck down the ability of states to regulate *interstate* railroad traffic, Congress stepped in. The Interstate Commerce Act of 1887 put common law principles and lessons from the state commissions into law. It required just and reasonable rates, prohibited rate discrimination for similarly situated shippers, prohibited undue or unreasonable preferences or advantages, required interconnection with other railroads, prevented cartels, and prohibited charging more for short distances than long ones. Rates also had to be filed publicly with the newly created Interstate Commerce Commission (ICC).

In its early years, the ICC was largely ineffective, but over
time, Congress further strengthened the law. It passed the
Hepburn Act of 1906, which allowed the ICC to set maximum
rates and strengthened the commission's enforcement capabilities. It put pipelines and railroad terminals under the ICC's
jurisdiction. And it created a structural separation in the "com-
modities clause" that prohibited railroads from shipping the
goods of companies that they also owned. This was an exten-
sion of the principle that was applied in the telephone and carriage company case. Without a structural separation, a railroad
that owned a coal company could, for example, give preference
to its own coal over competitors' coal. During World War I, the
Wilson administration nationalized the railroads. After the war,
Congress sought to return them to private hands, but it also
saw the great benefits that came from running the railroads as
a single, unified system. The Transportation Act of 1920 tried
to integrate the railroads to a much greater degree than before,
including through consolidation and rate-setting that focused
on the health of the system.

By the 1930s, the American tradition of regulated capitalism had coalesced into an approach that combined a set of structural regulatory goals and tools. Rather than simply require a
utility to serve all comers, the government could require universal service, so that everyone within the utility's geography
would get access—and it could prevent firms from entering and
exiting the market, to eliminate cream-skimming and loss of
service. Rather than simply posting prices publicly or determining that prices were just and reasonable, commissions could
instead investigate what it cost to provide a service, and require

36   a utility to charge cost plus a reasonable return on investment. And rather than simply require nondiscrimination between users, the law prohibited infrastructural firms from becoming conglomerates and operating downstream businesses. These structural separations ensured that the platform offered a level playing field to all users. This emergent model was distinctively American. It was neither exclusive public ownership nor *laissez-faire*. The American way was to ensure that the infrastructure for capitalism was regulated.

Advocates for the American tradition thought that regulation along these lines would serve many public-spirited goals. Structural regulation would ensure robust and reliable service. It would prevent destructive competition and price wars that impeded capital investment. It would stop monopoly and oligopoly harms like higher prices and favoritism. It would ensure a level playing field for all users, including by ensuring access to the service. For all these reasons it would also help expand commercial activity and facilitate economic growth.

Importantly, the American tradition recognized that regulation would help sustain democracy. Regulation would prevent the concentration of economic power into the hands of a small number of monopolists. And because economic power so often bleeds into political power, it would protect America's republican form of government from descending into oligarchy. Finally, regulation was seen as critical to national security. This was not simply because robust and reliable service is the foundation for national economic power, but also because, in a crisis, many of these businesses—transportation, energy, communications, banking—are critical for fighting and winning wars.

The Rise of Airline Regulation

After the airmail fiasco, Congress created a commission in 1934 to make recommendations on the future of airline regulation. In January 1935, the Federal Aviation Commission issued its report. Unsurprisingly, its recommendations channeled the American tradition of regulated capitalism. The Aviation Commission's vision was one of regulated competition: "It should be the general policy to preserve competition in the interest of improved service and technological development, while avoiding uneconomical paralleling of routes or duplication of facilities." In other words, the Commission wanted to prevent the kind of destructive competition that had dominated in the early years of the industry. The Commission explained that competition had been valuable to spur development, but that competition along each route was not what mattered. "If an airline running from coast to coast acquires faster and more comfortable airplanes, it takes but a little time for the patrons of a line running up and down the Mississippi Valley to complain if it fails to make the same advances." The Commission thus rejected the "common rule in Europe," of creating a "national monopoly . . . under close government supervision." The Commission also did not recommend a single private company serve as a regulated monopoly. As the Commission put it: "[T]oo much competition can be as bad as too little."

By 1938, members of Congress were ready to act. After more than a decade of flux in the airline industry, they were determined to create a system of regulation that would encourage the development of a stable, well-functioning airline industry. As Senator Patrick McCarran said:

38

> [T]here was never anything before this country more vital from the standpoint of national development, particularly at this hour of the world's history, and at this hour in our national history, than the legislation which is now pending before this subcommittee, because we are dealing with an infant industry, and we are dealing with it from the standpoint of what it can do for this country commercially, industrially, and as an arm of national defense.

When the Senate and House acted in 1938, both bodies explained the purposes of the landmark airline legislation. The Senate Commerce Committee's report described the goals of the bill this way:

> The recognized and accepted principles of the regulation of public utilities, as applied to other forms of transportation, have been incorporated in [the bill]. The committee feels that this bill will not only promote an orderly development of our Nation's civil aeronautics, but by its immediate enactment prevent the spread of bad practices and of destructive and wasteful tactics resulting from the intense competition now existing within the air-carrier industry.

The House Committee on Interstate and Foreign Commerce explained that the law was needed to "stabilize the air-transportation industry." A new, single regulator would solve problems of coordination between the ICC, Commerce, and Post Office. It agreed that existing law had also been designed for mail carriage, not economic stability.

Routes are awarded not upon the basis of the ability of the particular air carrier to perform the service or the requirements of the public convenience and necessity, but upon the letting of air-mail contracts to the lowest responsible bidders. This system has completely broken down in recent months, because the air carriers, in their desire to secure the right to carry the mail over a new route, have made absurdly low bids, indeed, have virtually evinced a willingness to pay for the privilege of carrying the mail over a particular route. A route once secured, however, under the existing system of air-mail contracts does not protect the air carrier operating that route from possible cutthroat competition, for air carriers are not required to secure a certificate or other authorization from the Government before beginning operations, other than one based upon safety requirements. Nor, is there any authority in the Federal Government under existing law to prevent competing carriers from engaging in rate wars which would be disastrous to all concerned.

The result of this chaotic situation of the air carriers has been to shake the faith of the investing public in their financial stability and to prevent the flow of funds into the industry.

The new legislation prohibited the operation of an aircraft as a common carrier without a "certificate of public convenience and necessity," required a certificate for flying a route, and regulated rates and other practices. It eliminated the existing mail contract system and allowed any airline to carry mail. The law

40   aimed to enable airlines to "operate on a stable basis" and "eliminate cutthroat competition among themselves." Importantly, financially secure airlines would also have little reason to compromise on safety standards.

The Civil Aeronautics Act and its Operation

The landmark Civil Aeronautics Act of 1938 created a system that followed the American tradition of regulated capitalism. The law created a Civil Aeronautics Authority (later renamed the Civil Aeronautics Board, or CAB), which would oversee the airline industry, including by determining entry into the airline sector and regulating rates to ensure they were just and reasonable. The law also provided for structural separations to prevent airlines from leveraging their power into owning and operating other business. It was truly a system—an integrated set of components that together would provide reliable service to the whole country.

First and foremost, under the regulated system, a person couldn't just start a new airline. To do so required permission from the CAB. The CAB restricted entry into the airline sector by authorizing carriers to operate along specified routes. Entry-restriction had important benefits. Limiting the number of carriers and the routes on which they flew would prevent destructive competition and wasted capital—akin to preventing hundreds of firms from trying to build telephone poles and wires. This would ensure that the industry would grow and develop in a reliable fashion and that investors would want to put their money into the industry. Limiting the number of carriers and assigning them routes also meant that the CAB could guarantee service to smaller and mid-sized communities.

Airlines would get some high-traffic, highly profitable routes and some less profitable ones, and they would cross-subsidize between them. Entry restriction also prevented new airlines from cream-skimming the highly profitable routes, which would ultimately leave the less profitable areas without service at all. This approach adapted the "post office principle" to airlines.

Modeled on regulatory systems in other transportation areas, the CAB evaluated air carriers to make sure they were "fit, willing, and able" to fly, and that any new flight route was "required by the public convenience and necessity." The first requirement ensured that air carriers would be able to serve the public reliably on their routes. The second requirement was designed to navigate between open entry in air transportation (which would lead to destructive competition) and monopoly abuses (by allowing new entry when necessary).

The two-part statutory criteria led to a two-step process at the CAB: to decide whether there was a market need, and to determine which airline received the route. The CAB weighed multiple criteria when determining public convenience and necessity for new routes: whether new services were based on public need, whether they could be adequately served by existing routes or carriers, whether new service would negatively impact other aspects of the system, and whether the benefits outweighed any costs the government might incur. As between carriers, the CAB again weighed multiple factors, ranging from route integration and frequency of service; to the type of plane and fare to be charged; to whether the airline needed its network strengthened, the possibility of harming other carriers economically, and the profitability of the route.

42   While the CAB recognized that it was neither to freeze entry altogether nor to adopt open entry, from the start it tended toward the former policy. Under the law, the CAB had to issue grandfather certificates to existing carriers—but it also simultaneously denied new entrants flight routes. This gave the major airlines a leg up from the start. It was also predictable. As Walter Brown had observed, the legacy carriers already had the expertise and track record to provide quality service.

After World War II, there was an excess of trained airline pilots, and as irregular (non-scheduled, non-certified) flights began to proliferate, the CAB began to tighten entry restriction and increase enforcement to prevent cream-skimming by the non-scheduled airlines. Throughout the 1950s and 1960s, the airline industry comprised "trunk" carriers and local service carriers. For the most part, trunk carriers flew between larger cities and on longer-haul routes. Local service carriers provided flights to small cities in a specific geography. The CAB allocated routes within each category. This approach worked relatively well. While local service carriers continued to receive some subsidies for service provision, by 1953, ten of the thirteen trunk carriers no longer needed government support. By the late 1950s, the industry had stabilized and was seeing record earnings.

In the mid-1950s, the CAB focused on competition and cut the number of city-pairs (that is, routes) without competition from forty to sixteen within only eighteen months. But even with more competition between carriers, the CAB tended toward maintaining a regulated oligopoly in the skies. In fact, it failed to authorize a single new entrant from 1950 to 1974.

The biggest airlines in the 1970s were the same as those in 1938. Part of the reason the CAB did not authorize new entrants was that it viewed each route as a market. It increased competition by expanding the routes of existing carriers, rather than authorizing new carriers. In line with this principle, the CAB system reshaped the industry's structure. While the four biggest airlines had nearly 82 percent market share in 1939, their market share had dropped to 58.6 percent by 1972. Meanwhile, the other "trunk" line carriers doubled their collective market share during the CAB regime, from 17.7 percent in 1939 to 33 percent in 1972.

In order to prevent airlines from abusing their power, the Civil Aeronautics Act both included nondiscrimination rules and empowered the CAB to engage in rate regulation—setting and regulating airfares in order to prevent unjust and unreasonable pricing. The nondiscrimination provisions mandated that airlines could not give any "undue or unreasonable preference or advantage to any particular person, port, locality, or description of traffic" or subject them to "any unjust discrimination or any undue or unreasonable prejudice or disadvantage in any respect whatsoever." This provision ensured that airlines didn't offer different services or prices to identical individuals, and offered cities protection from unfair and inadequate service.

With respect to prices, the CAB's application of nondiscrimination principles changed over time. In the 1940s and 1950s, the primary worry was that airlines would fail or need subsidies. The CAB therefore monitored rates but did not adopt industrywide fare regulations because the airlines agreed to lower prices. With an increasingly stable industry in the

44   late 1950s, the CAB initiated an investigation to determine rates across the industry. The investigation was designed as a judicial-style process, and it took four years to complete. Over the course of the 1960s, the CAB wanted to expand the size of the market of air travel, so it authorized discounted fares to spur more demand.

While the details changed over time, generally speaking, the CAB followed the traditional formula for rate regulation that applied across network, platform, and utility industries: the airline's costs plus a reasonable return on investment would yield a revenue requirement. From this, the CAB would determine a price per mile. Airlines would then charge equal fares for equal miles. A 500-mile flight would therefore cost less than a 1,000-mile flight, and two 750-mile flights would cost the same—even if one route was more popular than another.

Importantly, this pricing system allowed airlines to invest in new innovations, particularly "designing and buying even bigger, faster, and more exciting airplanes." The development of jet technology in the mid- to late-1950s, for example, had brought with it massive new investments into aircraft. Of course, new technological investments also meant higher costs, so airlines were taking on higher debt levels and earning lower returns. But the system of rate regulation was designed to address and facilitate technological innovation. The CAB could simply authorize rate increases to cover these costs—and it ultimately set an industry standard rate of return based on a target load factor of 63 percent (that is, an assumption that planes fly 63 percent full).

Finally, the Civil Aeronautics Act prevented airlines from owning other businesses. It had a range of "structural

separations" rules to prevent airlines from leveraging power
from one area into another. Airlines could not own or operate
any other business in the aviation sector. Executives and board
members of the airlines couldn't serve simultaneously on the
boards of other businesses in the aviation sector either. These
provisions ensured that airlines were focused on flying—and
that they would not use their privileged status and guaranteed
revenue to monopolize other aspects of the industry.

The CAB and the Economic Crisis of the 1970s

The regulated system built a strong and reliable airline industry in the post–World War II era. But by the late 1960s and early
1970s, the airlines faced a threefold crisis. First, while passenger travel was growing swiftly in the 1960s, it slowed around
1970. At the same time, manufacturers started delivering new,
wide-bodied jets. These were a technological marvel, but they
also increased costs for airlines and simultaneously led to
excess capacity. Bigger planes and less demand meant emp-
tier flights. By 1971, load factors were averaging merely 48 percent. Costs were up too. Between 1969 and 1978, jet fuel prices
increased by a whopping 222 percent. After the oil shocks in
1973, prices spiked. The Nixon administration initially explored
cutting the use of jet fuel by one-third per day. The FAA rejected
that idea. The administration then proposed a 15 percent cut
within two months. The industry pushed back. Airlines ultimately agreed to cut their fuel usage by 5 percent. The combination of these developments meant the CAB would again have to
increase prices.

In 1969, the industry asked the CAB to do just that. The
CAB first attempted to determine a new rate structure by

46 negotiating informally with the industry. But the CAB got taken to court for conducting a closed-door proceeding. So the CAB then announced that it would set rates industrywide through a new, more transparent process. Under the "Domestic Passenger Fare Investigation," the CAB would first consider the costs and revenues on an industrywide basis, assuming a load factor of 55 percent. It then added a 12 percent return on investment to the costs. Fares were set in order to meet this level of revenue. The CAB would recalculate the figures every three months based on updated data. This process proved administrable and also made it easy for firms to predict which rates would be approved as "just and reasonable." At the same time, this approach had problems. In addition to its built-in assumptions (about load factors and the need for a specific, fixed, industrywide return on investment), the model did not consider that demand for air travel was elastic: by lowering fares, airlines might actually draw new travelers, fill seats, and expand routes.

The CAB chairman from 1969 to 1973 also sought to address the crisis in the airline industry by reducing excess capacity. He approved carrier agreements to reduce the number of flights on some routes. He also imposed an almost total moratorium on new routes (only two new routes were approved between 1969 and 1974). Unable to compete on price, with new routes, or with more flights on the same routes, airlines shifted to competing over quality of service on airplanes. Lounges on airplanes came first, then further amenities. "When American installed piano bars, TWA countered with electronic draw-poker machines." Delta added steak and champagne; Continental served complimentary Chivas Regal in coach.

While the system of airline regulation had much to offer, the challenges of the late 1960s and early 1970s created an opportunity for policy change. The CAB adopted reasonable policies to address the challenges facing the airlines, but with the side effect of incentivizing eye-popping competition over services. The stage was set for a swift assault on the regulatory system—and for its collapse.

The Decline and Fall of Airline Regulation

The deregulation of the airline industry was one of the swiftest, most thoroughgoing policy changes in American history. In a few short years, the airline industry went from being tightly regulated by the CAB to fully competitive. The story of deregulation involves new ideas, policy entrepreneurship, bipartisan political alignment, and aggressive bureaucratic action.

"Let's Get Rid of the CAB"

By the 1970s, the intellectual context for regulation had shifted considerably. Economists and legal scholars, especially those associated with the "Chicago School," had attacked the reasoning behind the American tradition of regulated capitalism. The Chicago School and its allies generally thought that markets were mostly the same—that there weren't big differences between utilities or infrastructure and ordinary goods like mugs or T-shirts. As a result, they believed that competition was viable in many industries that the American tradition had understood for centuries as tending toward monopoly

or oligopoly. They were skeptical of government regulation
as a way to accomplish economic goals, even if those goals
were about promoting commerce and industry; safeguarding
national security, encouraging labor peace and economic security; or ensuring geographic equality and service. And they were
strongly against price or rate regulation, even when the purpose
was to ensure uniform rates and universal access to utility-like
services. Instead, the Chicago School economists and their
allies believed that the law should track economic theory—and
should focus on efficiency, even if that sacrificed these other
goals. In the airline context, perhaps the most important works
in this vein were academic studies arguing that fares would be
lower without regulation. With rising inflation and fuel shortages in the 1970s, this line of argumentation and research
appeared to offer a solution to the problem of high airline prices.

The neoliberal turn in economics might not have spurred
such a dramatic regulatory change had it not overlapped with
the views and ambitions of *liberal* policy entrepreneurs in
Washington, DC. For years, consumer activist Ralph Nader
had argued that federal government agencies were "captured"
by the industries they regulated. Rather than helping consumers, the agencies largely did the bidding of the industry.
Nader's argument aligned with research and advocacy from
the Chicago School, which had argued that industry demanded
regulation and regulation served industry. This new, liberal
critique of regulation thus overlapped with the rising conser-
vative movement's objection to federal government action.
President Gerald Ford, for example, argued that airline deregulation would reduce "big government" and help promote free
enterprise.

50   Two of the most important players in deregulation were then—Harvard law school professor and later—Supreme Court justice Stephen Breyer and Democratic senator Ted Kennedy. Kennedy asked Breyer to help him find topics to help bolster his reputation as a serious policymaker. At a Transportation Department meeting with airline executives in 1974, Breyer watched as the secretary of transportation asked why the airlines wouldn't raise prices to address their economic challenges. The thirty-six-year-old antitrust professor concluded in that moment that the airlines were "a cartel, a simple cartel being organized by the government." Breyer proposed deregulating the airlines to Kennedy. The senator liked the politics because the splashy initiative could be framed as both consumer friendly and anti—big government. The youthful Breyer, meanwhile, was eager to take bold action. His pitch to potential staffer Phil Bakes, a twenty-eight-year-old who would go on to hold many important positions in the airline industry, was, "Let's get rid of the CAB."

     Breyer and Bakes seem to have been motivated not just by economics but also by the atmosphere of scandal around Nixon and Watergate. Nixon's Committee to Re-elect the President had asked airline executives to donate money to his 1972 campaign. Two airlines made illegal campaign contributions to Nixon's reelection, were discovered, and the executives were held accountable. Bakes recruited William Gingery, a thirty-six-year-old CAB staffer, to secretly copy government documents on anticompetitive practices and give them to his investigative team. But Gingery discovered in the process that many more airlines had slush funds, like the ones implicated in the Nixon scandal, and that the CAB had closed out the investigation without exposing them. Rather than testify in the Senate and feeling betrayed by the CAB superiors he had once held in high regard, Gingery shot and killed himself. The entire affair was referred to the Watergate prosecutors, who concluded that Gingery committed suicide and closed the case.

In 1974–75, Kennedy and Breyer held a series of congressional hearings on the airline industry, leading to a blockbuster 1975 report calling for deregulation. Airline deregulation was thus an early example of the emerging anti-regulation ideology that both Democrats and Republicans would ultimately embrace. The Kennedy subcommittee's investigation focused on whether the CAB's operations had "led to 'adequate, economical and efficient service by air carriers at reasonable charges.'" The subcommittee summarized its indictment of the CAB this way:

> [C]lassical route-award and ratemaking procedures ha[ve] brought about fares that are far too high. The airline industry is potentially highly competitive, but the Board's system of regulation discourages the airlines from competing in price and virtually forecloses new firms from entering the industry. . . . [T]he airlines—prevented from competing in price—simply channel their competitive energies toward costlier service: more flights, more planes, more frills. . . .
>
> The remedy is for the Board to allow both new and existing firms greater freedom to lower fares and greater freedom to obtain new routes. This freedom should lead the airlines to offer service in fuller planes at substantially lower prices, a form of service that most consumers desire.

52   The subcommittee criticized CAB's policies and practices in area after area. It observed that Congress had not intended to freeze entry into the airline sector altogether, but wanted "a cautious, but moderately liberal, policy allowing new firms to enter the industry as the market for air travel expanded." Yet from 1950 to 1974, seventy-nine firms applied to the CAB for entry and the CAB granted zero applications.

The subcommittee concluded that the CAB's administrative practices were unfair. The CAB's standards were generally opaque in route cases, and the 1969–1974 moratorium on new routes had been ordered by the chair, without notice or a public hearing. At the start of 1975, the subcommittee found that more than two-thirds of route applications had been pending for at least two years and a quarter had been pending for more than five years.[*]

The CAB's ratemaking system was also thought to be flawed, as it had led to planes flying with too many empty seats and fierce competition over amenities and service but not price. Rate regulation, including the system of equal fares for equal miles, the subcommittee argued, did "not produce 'cost-related' fares." The subcommittee was also outraged that the CAB had refused to approve proposed across-the-board price cuts by one airline because the reduction, under the rate regulation system, would have interactive effects on the rest of the industry. Of course, this was precisely the point of the regulated system: to produce uniform fares that cross-subsidized some routes.

[*] Recall that this was a deliberate moratorium policy adopted to address low load-factors.

Fundamentally, the subcommittee objected to structural regulation in the airline sector. "In the subcommittee's view there is no substantial historical, empirical, or logical reason for believing that increased reliance upon competition would lead to predatory pricing, destructive competition, or risk of monopolization."* The subcommittee said that "the airline industry is not a 'natural monopoly'; it is 'structurally competitive.'" So confident were the authors in this conclusion that they predicted that "the industry may be able to support as many as 200 efficient airline companies."

To support its position, the subcommittee addressed possible counterarguments. It attributed industry instability in the 1920s and 1930s not to economic dynamics, but to airmail subsidies. "There was never a period in which market forces led to 'destructive competition' or 'industry chaos.'" The low bids and predatory pricing that emerged immediately prior to the 1938 Act were primarily a function of low consumer demand due to the Great Depression and bad publicity from the Black hearings, coupled with the ability of the ICC to raise fares.

The subcommittee also concluded that the airline sector was not and would not be subject to predatory pricing. Experts "told the subcommittee that these conditions do not exist in the airline industry." The subcommittee analogized airlines to hardware stores and grocery stores, noting that those industries do not face destructive competition, despite

---

* Predatory pricing is when a firm undercuts the price of another firm, at below the cost of the good or service. It can occur during destructive competition, when firms are competing to win the market, or when a monopolist or oligopolist firm is trying to push out new competitors. The winner in these situations can then raise prices afterward.

54   a possible benefit to selling goods below cost to win market share. Businesses, it said, recognize they have to cover their fixed costs. If anything, the subcommittee claimed, regulation *led to* predatory pricing because it made it difficult for new airlines to enter the market.

The subcommittee also dismissed a "more sophisticated" argument—one that has particular resonance in the post-COVID context. The argument was that the airline industry is cyclical based on demand. When demand is low, airlines cut back. To cover their fixed costs, they are eventually forced to ground aircraft, reduce service, and fire employees. When demand increases, the airlines have to rehire employees, un-ground aircraft, and start service again. Those who saw the industry as defined by this cycle observed that regulation prevents the wasteful destruction of jobs (and economic value) by mitigating some of the initial price competition and by maintaining stability in crisis periods. The subcommittee rejected this interpretation for two reasons: it argued that this is not what happened in the 1930s and that, in any case, those dynamics were possible under regulation as well.

As evidence of the promise of competition, the subcommittee looked to California and Texas. The Civil Aeronautics Act only applied to *interstate* flights, and both California and Texas had substantial *intrastate* air traffic in the mid-twentieth century. Because intrastate traffic was not regulated by the CAB, the subcommittee thought it offered evidence of what a deregulated system might look like. Drawing on academic studies, the subcommittee noted that airline tickets were about half the price on similar-length routes in those states, as compared to interstate routes regulated by the CAB. The subcommittee dismissed alternative explanations for this price differential, including good weather in those states, high traffic density along the routes, the costs of interlining (connections to other destinations), different aircraft types, and the regulatory requirement to cover higher-cost routes.

The subcommittee also addressed the criticism that deregulation would undermine geographic access to air service. Opponents of deregulation held that airlines cross-subsidized routes: higher-traffic, high profit routes enabled the airline to subsidize lower-traffic, low profit routes. The result was that airlines could offer "equal fares for equal miles," per CAB policy. The benefit of this approach, opponents claimed, was to ensure service to smaller markets. The subcommittee responded first that "pure cross subsidy simply does not exist to any significant extent." Competition was so severe, the subcommittee thought, that carriers had no money left for subsidies.* In addition, small community service is profitable because those routes feed into broader networks, giving additional value to the airline.† In any event, the subcommittee also found that "if cross-subsidy did exist, it would not be desirable." Why, the subcommittee asked, should a grandmother traveling across the country subsidize a businessman going between small airports? Finally, cross-subsidies were "politically invisible." A better system, it thought, was for Congress to decide how much to subsidize service.

---

* Of course, if that is true, it is hard to see how carriers were able to fund extravagant services like piano bars.

† Note that this is an argument about network effects and scale, which is in tension with the claim that the sector is structurally competitive.

56   In response to these challenges and findings, the subcommittee made a number of recommendations. It concluded that incremental reforms were not viable: "Defects in airline regulation run so deep that major change is required . . . reliance upon strong safety regulation, the antitrust laws to prevent predatory behavior, and the competitive process is more appropriate." At the same time, it advised "a program of gradual, measured change toward increased reliance upon competition." To address process concerns, changes "should take place only after adequate opportunity is given both to members of the industry and the general public to submit views and arguments." The subcommittee recommended that the CAB begin liberalizing entry to remove route restrictions, liberalize charter rules, and eventually allow entry for any carrier that is "fit, willing, and able." Carriers should also have the power to "charge the prices they desire" and "introduce systems of price discounts that reflect cost differences."

The Deregulatory Moment

Two years after the Kennedy report, President Jimmy Carter appointed Alfred Kahn to run the CAB. Kahn was a Cornell University economics professor, whose book *The Economics of Regulation* (1970) advanced a vision that was skeptical of the American tradition of regulated capitalism. Kahn's foundation was that buyers should have to pay the marginal cost for goods and services. Policies that enabled cross-subsidies, uniform pricing, and regulated rates for utilities were therefore anathema to Kahn's worldview. In 1974, Kahn became chair of the New York Public Service Commission, the state's utility regulator, where he brought this approach to reforming electricity and telephone prices. Kahn famously believed that it was bad for the telephone company to offer directory assistance because each user didn't pay for the use of the service.

At the CAB, Kahn's predecessor, a lawyer named John Robson, had already ended the route moratorium and anticompetitive agreements that limited capacity, but Robson had felt constrained by the statute from taking more radical measures. At the helm of the CAB, the economist Kahn pushed harder and faster. The statute provided that CAB issue certificates when "required by public convenience and necessity," a provision that was intended to restrict entry to prevent both destructive competition and possible monopolization. Kahn's CAB authorized any low-fare proposal presented to the Board, made low fares a virtually determinative criteria for entry, allowed for downward departures of fares by 70 percent, and adopted an experimental policy called "multiple permissive entry," under which carriers could enter new routes. Objections to these policies came from a number of directions: there were fears that Kahn was moving too fast; that ad hoc changes might have unpredictable effects; and that destructive competition would lead to lower industry profits and long-term oligopoly. For his part, Kahn said, "I feel like the Red Queen of *Alice in Wonderland*, executing the sentence first, then getting around to holding the trial."

Notably, there weren't marquee battles over Kahn's actions in the courts. Paul Stephen Dempsey, one of the leading scholars and critics of airline deregulation (and himself a CAB lawyer in the late 1970s), has observed that Kahn pursued two strategies to insulate the CAB's deregulatory revolution. First, recognizing that its actions were potentially contrary to the law's entry restriction provisions, the CAB acted swiftly across multiple

58   areas at once. If the courts reversed one action "here or there," it "would not diminish significantly the overall impact of the mass of decisions." In any case, it would take years for litigation to reach final decisions. The goal was to "scramble the eggs" so they could not be put back together after the fact. Second, the CAB gave interested parties a chance to comment on each policy decision, and the Board took care to explain away those comments. This made it harder to win a case challenging those decisions in court. Of course, Kahn had one other thing going for him: the Kennedy report. Even if his actions were contrary to the intentions of the 1938 Congress that passed the law, he was acting in accordance with the preferences of powerful legislators in 1978.

Kahn's actions ratified some of the innovative practices already taking place in the airline industry. Robert Crandall, the head of marketing and later CEO of American Airlines, determined in 1976 that airlines need not charge uniform fares for seats. Once the plane's costs were covered, the cost of additional passengers was extremely low. American thus began offering "Super Saver" fares to fill those seats. These lower-priced seats upset American's most loyal customers, so Crandall eventually invented a frequent flyer loyalty program to give them additional benefits. Airlines were also in the midst of developing computer reservation services (CRS), by which travel agents could search for and book flights. United was first, but it was Crandall's emphatic performance at a trade show for travel agents that made American's Sabre system the industry leader. Meanwhile, Frank Lorenzo, head of the small Texas International, came up with the idea of launching no-frills, no-meals (only peanuts) service. His new "Peanuts" fares rolled out in 1977, and immediately sold out.

With radical changes already underway, Congress stepped in and passed the Airline Deregulation Act of 1978. The debate over the act replicated many of the issues that had surfaced during the Kennedy investigation. Senator Howard Cannon (D-NV) argued that the airline industry "clearly does not have the characteristics of public utilities" and that "no community will lose air service as a result of this bill." Senator Charles Percy (R-IL) declared that "there are few, if any, economies of scale of any great importance in the airline industry." Senator Barry Goldwater of Arizona, who had been the Republican nominee for president in 1964, objected to deregulation, predicting:

> In the short term, it is reasonable to expect more flights, lower fares, and lower load factors as airlines exercise their rights of automatic entry. Over the long term, there will be a shake out in the industry through mergers or bankruptcies. Then, competition will decrease, load factors will go up, and fares will rise to a point where airlines can make a reasonable return on invested capital.

Importantly, with the exception of United, the other major airlines—even the most innovative ones—were fiercely opposed to deregulation. Lorenzo thought deregulation would kill off small airlines like his. During a hearing, he said to Senator Cannon that the result would be "a couple of large airlines." And when asked if deregulation would be "an attack on the labor movement," Lorenzo agreed that it would be. Even more strikingly, American's Bob Crandell approached Bakes after a hearing, saying, "You fucking academic pinhead! You don't know shit. You can't deregulate this industry, you're going to wreck it.

60   You don't know a goddamn thing!" He then walked off in a huff, leaving Bakes stunned and wondering who the man was.

The final version of the Airline Deregulation Act largely tracked the analysis and policy objectives in the Kennedy report. Deregulating entry would bring price and service competition. Rather than "requiring" that a service meet the standard of public convenience and necessity, the 1978 Act now required the CAB to issue certificates "consistent with" public convenience and necessity. That minor edit was enough to enable competition and end the system of restricted entry. The requirement that an airline be "fit, willing, and able" remained unchanged. Within sixty days of the law's passage, dormant routes (those that were authorized but did not have frequent weekly service) would also be awarded to the first carrier that applied. The law also planned for a gradual six-year liberalization process. The CAB would continue to license routes based on public convenience and necessity until the end of 1981; it would have power over rates until 1983; and it would make fitness determinations until the end of 1984. On January 1, 1985, licensing for fitness determinations and other responsibilities (consumer protection, international issues, and merger review, for example) would transfer to the Department of Transportation. The CAB would then be dissolved.

Implementing Deregulation

At this point, President Carter moved Kahn to the White House to help fight inflation. Under new leadership, the CAB took aggressive action to deregulate the industry. Lawyers for the carriers lined up even before the deregulation bill was signed, awaiting their chance to get access to dormant routes. Within a month of passage, some 238 routes had been awarded. The CAB also immediately confronted the question of whether to allow any qualified carriers to serve a market. It declared its broad support for an open entry system, even though it chose initially not to settle all questions at once.

But in case after case, the CAB's consistent approach was swift deregulation to allow new carriers and new routes. In one instance, Alaska Airlines argued that allowing open entry into southeastern Alaska would create competition that would ultimately lead to "a reduction or loss of service to the southeast Alaska communities and bush points." The CAB dismissed this concern. It claimed that Alaska Airlines was simply seeking protectionism over these routes:

> We recognize that the greater reliance we now place on competition . . . means that airlines will be increasingly less willing and able to cross-subsidize loss operations with monopoly profits on other routes. Our 1971 decision in the *Alaska Service Investigation*, 58 C.A.B. 389 (1972), which established the current pattern of Seattle-Southeast Alaska authority, granted [Alaska Airlines] a temporary monopoly essentially on cross-subsidy grounds—i.e., that it was willing to serve both the lucrative and marginal (or worse) markets, while Western [Airlines] was only interested in the profitable ones. We no longer consider this a valid reason for restricting competition.[*]

---

[*] The fact that the Board's decision in 1971 was based on cross-subsidies is contrary to the subcommittee's claim that there were no cross-subsidies built into the system.

62   When an applicant airline trying to get into a market conceded that the route's volume could only support one carrier,
the CAB still awarded multiple entry. Nor did the CAB consider limited airport terminal space a valid reason for restricting
entry. The Board would not narrow its policy to "avoid practical
problems that new entrants could pose to airport authorities. . . .
We are not now inclined to deny entry to any qualified applicant
simply in order to avoid airport congestion."

During the proceedings in these cases and others, parties raised a variety of concerns about predatory pricing and
destructive competition. Small carriers argued that the big airlines would price at the cost of service and losses would drive
the small carriers out of business. There were fears that if a
low-cost carrier entered markets with financially secure airlines, the latter would simply match prices to drive them out.
The result would be monopolization and oligopoly. The Board
rejected these concerns, believing instead that economies of
scale were not a significant feature of the industry.

In 1979, concerns about the Board's approach hit a boiling
point when CAB member Richard J. O'Melia began to dissent
vigorously and repeatedly. In "Austin/San Antonio-Atlanta,"
he dissented because "the Board . . . is unnecessarily and . . .
woodenly" trying "to bring about deregulation today rather
than after the transition period prescribed by Congress, and
because it appears more concerned with the doctrinal concept
of competition than with the real-world demands of air service." Still, the CAB's innovations continued. Traditionally, the
CAB considered entry awards by looking at particular routes.
In the *Milwaukee Show-Cause Proceeding*, the Board took a new
approach: it "tentatively decided to grant all applications filed

by 'qualified' carriers for any conceivable domestic route with
which Milwaukee could be linked." O'Melia again issued a stren-
uous dissent:

> What is the effect, what are the consequences of this unre-
> strained carnival of route giving? There are two conse-
> quences that particularly concern me. The first is that
> rather than the phased and orderly transition to deregu-
> lation that Congress mandated, the clear meaning of the
> Board's action here is instant deregulation. . . .
>
> The second . . . is that we are unnecessarily, improp-
> erly and in a very shameful manner destroying one of the
> strengths of an administrative agency like the Board—its
> quasi-judicial nature and function. The shameful part is
> that the destruction is being carried out not with clean
> direct surgical strokes, but by draining out the reason for
> being of our judicial process. With no facts to be analyzed,
> with no law to be interpreted and followed, what is the
> point of having a judicial process? . . .
>
> This gutting of our judicial process, this mockery of
> evidentiary hearings, combined with the telescoping
> of the transition period, is not, in my opinion, what the
> Airline Deregulation Act contemplates. I can't believe
> that this is what Congress had in mind. And I feel ever so
> strongly that this is not in the best interest of the consum-
> ers, the carriers, and the communities of our country.

The CAB also reformed the process of evaluating whether
an applicant was "fit, willing, and able" to fly in order to align
that provision with the aim of multiple permissive entry.

64   Traditionally, the Board considered a variety of factors, including whether airlines had a secure financial position, an insured fleet, maintenance operations, qualified management, and a willingness to provide for the public. The Board now revised this standard, requiring merely that an applicant show they had a *plan* for getting financing, a *proposal* for satisfactory operations, would have managerial and technical capabilities *before* flying, and would comply with the law. O'Melia dissented here too. "From this day forward," he said, "an aspiring entrepreneur need only show that in a set of perfect circumstances the proposed operations could be feasible."

Over these and other similar dissents, the Board swiftly brought the deregulation of the airline industry—well in advance of the statutory timeline for deregulation. In three years, the industry effectively went from regulated to deregulated.

The Contradictions and Challenges of the Deregulatory Vision

While airline deregulation offered a forceful critique of the regulated system, it also suffered from a range of internal contradictions and evidentiary challenges. The overall drive for deregulation seems, forty-five years later, to have been as much a function of ideological motivations as logical ones. Identifying these problems is critical to understanding the broader failures of airline deregulation.

Consider first a series of contradictions. Advocates for deregulation dismissed the policy of "equal fares for equal miles," which was intended to establish a system of cross-subsidies that would enable smaller markets to get affordable service. The subcommittee went so far as to claim that cross-subsidies

COLUMBIA GLOBAL REPORTS

Columbia Global Reports is a nonprofit publishing imprint from Columbia University that commissions authors to produce works of original thinking and on-site reporting from all over the world, on a wide range of topics.

Our books are short, but ambitious. They offer new ways of looking at and understanding the major issues of our time.

Most readers are curious and busy. Our books are for them.

GET 25% OFF YOUR NEXT BOOK!

Scan this QR code or visit **globalreports.columbia.edu/learn-more** to sign-up for our newsletter and receive 25% off your next Columbia Global Reports book.

did not exist as a way to ensure service to remote areas. But the
CAB itself had allocated routes and rates for precisely that reason. At the time of the hearings, United Airlines reported that
58 of their 327 city-pair routes were unprofitable. The subcommittee argued that United might still operate some of them
because of network effects, that abandoning some routes was
of no concern because they were of a short distance, and the
loss would likely be only 29 routes. In other words, the subcommittee admitted that there would be losses due to abandoning
cross-subsidies, while simultaneously arguing that there were
no cross-subsidies in the system.

The subcommittee also held that the airline industry was
"structurally competitive" and that it did not feature predatory
pricing, destructive competition, or serious barriers to entry.
At the same time, however, the subcommittee acknowledged
that there were network effects in airlines having many different
routes, including to smaller markets, because such routes would
expand the size and therefore value of the network. Critics of
deregulation worried that competitors would cream-skim the
most profitable routes, leaving the big carriers too little to cover
their overhead. The big carriers in turn would delay aircraft
replacements and other longer-term investments and worsen
their quality of service. The subcommittee rejected this concern. Rather,

> existing carriers may have a significant advantage. As they
> are quick to point out, providing a network of connected
> service is advantageous to travelers. Many travelers want
> to fly between two cities on a single plane with only one
> stop in between, or to fly on one airline with conveniently

scheduled connections; and they presumably would pay
        more for this service.

        If such network effects are so valuable, there are two import-
ant consequences. First, these network effects themselves act as
a barrier to entry. Consumers may prefer a large network, making it harder for a new entrant to operate competitively along
a single route. Second, network effects mean there are benefits
to industry consolidation because a larger firm can operate the
wider network. In either case, the market is not "structurally
competitive" and does not have minimal barriers to entry. The
argument about barriers to entry suffered from a third problem
as well. Airplanes have to take off and land somewhere, and airports have a limited number of runways and gates. But this barrier to entry was not a serious concern.

        The Air Transport Association (ATA)—the trade associ-
ation of airlines—argued at the time that deregulation would
lead to airlines abandoning unprofitable routes and to industry consolidation. Its model predicted that airlines would cur-
tail service, run extremely full flights, and abandon 373 nonstop
route segments in order to maximize profits. The subcommittee dismissed the ATA study as "fatally flawed" because it was
based on assumptions of monopoly or cartel operations, which
would be impossible under competition. "[I]t says little about
what would happen in the real world. In fact, the real world without regulation would not be inhabited by an airline monopolist
or a cartel. It would be a highly competitive world with flexible
prices, where planes could not fly 86.7 percent full on average,
and carriers could not earn $2 billion profit per year."

The subcommittee's interpretation of the evidence was also overly credulous when it supported their deregulatory views. For example, the subcommittee argued that low prices in California and Texas were a function of competition, not other factors. The academic study on which the report relied described California from 1946 to 1965 (after which the state imposed regulation on the sector). During that time, eighteen small carriers entered into the marketplace and sixteen left via mergers or bankruptcy. The subcommittee concluded that "[t]he obvious implication is that existing competition and the threat of new entry led different carriers to try different types of service at different prices; those airlines that could efficiently provide travelers with the service and price they wanted were successful; and travelers obtained the fuller-plane, low-fare service they desire." The subcommittee explained that predatory pricing and other destructive competition dynamics were not at issue because ten of these airlines did not last fifteen months and another failed. It is not clear why this evidence decisively helps the case for deregulation. To exclude ten airlines because they failed quickly and another because it failed slowly might suggest that the industry *is* subject to destructive competition and consolidation into a local oligopoly—rather than characterized by healthy competition.

The subcommittee also did not assess the possibility that the California and Texas systems had lower prices because they were themselves cream-skimming routes vis-à-vis federally regulated carriers. As we have seen, entry restriction is designed to prevent new entrants from capturing the highest value routes at a lower price (cream-skimming) and leaving others with the

68   higher cost routes. Because flights within California and Texas were unregulated, it is possible that prices were lower because airlines were not required to serve more remote and smaller markets out of state. In other words, in-state carriers could offer lower rates because they were cream-skimming the most profitable in-state routes.

Indeed, the evidence for this alternative explanation is strong. Herb Kelleher and Rollin King, who founded Air Southwest in Texas in 1966 (now Southwest Airlines), believed their airline would succeed *precisely because* it could undercut the federally regulated prices of national carriers. Federally regulated airlines Braniff and Trans Texas argued to the CAB and then in federal court that even though Southwest operated wholly in-state, it was stealing business from federally regulated competitors and impacting interstate commerce. As a result, they thought the CAB should have to license and regulate Southwest. Braniff and Trans Texas lost their lawsuit because the law explicitly said that federal regulation only applied to airlines traveling between states. But the lawsuit illustrated that the airlines themselves understood that cream-skimming means cheaper prices on the most trafficked routes—and higher prices on less-trafficked routes.

Ultimately, the internal contradictions of the deregulatory approach reflected a misguided view of the economic dynamics of the airline industry. Over the first decade of deregulation, this would become crystal clear.

The Great Debate
Did Deregulation Work?

Deregulation was a transformative, radical, sweeping policy. In just a few short years, the airline industry went from being structurally regulated—entry, routes, prices—to deregulated. According to its advocates, deregulating airlines was supposed to create competition, lower prices, and make everyone better off. Many people today have feelings about how airline deregulation worked. The conventional wisdom is that prices went down, and so deregulation was successful. But the real story is not so straightforward—and not so favorable to the champions of deregulation.

"The Closest Thing to War in Peacetime"
After deregulation, Texas International's Frank Lorenzo knew he had to act fast. He had feared deregulation, and he now believed that he urgently needed to have a bigger airline and to lower his costs. Bigger airlines not only had more routes but they could weather price wars. So Lorenzo immediately started looking for targets. He first bought up 9.2 percent of the much

70   bigger National Airlines, only to see Pan Am swoop in and take
it from him. But his failed attempt was itself a success: Lorenzo
made a killing as National's stock price jumped from the merger.
Other airlines recognized the value of size too. Pan Am bought
National. North Carolina and Southern joined. Alfred Kahn was
confused by these mergers. He wondered why airlines wanted to
get bigger instead of competing with each other. Over the objections of the Department of Justice, the CAB approved these
mergers. As one member said, it was time to "let the market
work."

Meanwhile, there was a rush of new entrants into the industry. There were former charter operators World Airways and
Capitol Airlines, and startups Columbia Air and Air Chicago.
The newly formed Air Muse was referred to as Air Revenge
because its founder created it after a falling-out with Southwest
chief Herb Kelleher. Frank Lorenzo also had a falling-out with
his longtime colleague and friend Don Burr. Upon leaving
Texas International, Burr took stock of his options. He recognized that the highest volume of flights was in the Boston to
Washington, DC, corridor. So he decided to start a new airline,
staffed by cheap, non-unionized workers, and to only serve
this high-volume region. Burr took over the crumbling Newark
airport, renovated it, and made it the headquarters for his
new low-cost, no-frills airline, People Express. Its first flights
started in 1981.

Lorenzo had noticed the same thing about the north-
east corridor. He reorganized Texas International into a holding company, Texas Air, and then started a competing low-cost,
no-frills, non-unionized airline, New York Air. Lorenzo secured
landing slots at La Guardia Airport in New York City and started

flying with repainted Texas International planes. Lorenzo's
actions upset his labor unions, who not only saw the danger of
a non-union shop in their corporate family but also of moving
valuable assets from unionized operations (Texas International)
to non-unionized (New York Air). Lorenzo also made some
splashy new hires. He put Kahn on his board; hired Phil Bakes,
who had just finished a stint as deputy campaign manager for
Kennedy's failed 1980 presidential bid; and brought in Mike
Levine, a top aide at the CAB whose enthusiasm for deregulation had gotten him the nickname "Ayatollah."

These new low-cost, no-frills, no-union airlines put considerable pressure on the big legacy carriers. The upstarts could
cream-skim routes and undercut the big carriers on price. But
the big airlines also had weapons. When the cheap upstarts
and even the older, distinguished Eastern Airlines started flying coast-to-coast routes, the big carriers matched them on
price. Eastern lost so much money that it exited the market.
World Airlines went bankrupt. People Express started flights
from Newark to Minneapolis-St. Paul, a Northwest hub, in
1983. Northwest responded not only by selling its flights below
People Express's prices, but it also used its size and volume to
sandwich People Express's flights on both sides. People Express
soon gave up.

American Airlines' Bob Crandall, now at the helm of the
company, played hardball too. When New York Air and Midway
Airlines started flying to Detroit, he said to his team, "I want 'em
out of Detroit." Sabre, American's computer reservation system (CRS), stopped listing New York Air at the top of its search
display results. New York Air's ticket sales plummeted because
travel agents couldn't see its flights. By late 1981, New York Air

72   had pulled out of the New York–Detroit market. American also started charging booking fees for using its CRS—but set the price for booking on a competitor airline higher, nudging people to stick with American. Other big carriers with CRS services engaged in similar practices—in addition to offering travel agents bonuses for booking with them. A few years later, the federal government took inspiration from the American tradition of regulated capitalism and imposed a nondiscrimination rule on CRS operations.

The big airlines looked for every possible way to strike back at the upstarts. In May 1981, Crandall rolled out a new frequent flyer system, with personal accounts and miles tracking. United matched American eleven days later. Rivals crowed at these frequent flyer perks, calling them anticompetitive kickbacks and a form of "white collar crime." In 1982, on a phone call with Braniff president Howard Putnam, Crandall suggested the two of them raise their prices simultaneously to stem losses from price wars. Putnam recorded the call, and he sent the tape to the Justice Department. Attempted price fixing was not technically a crime, so the Justice Department hit Crandall with attempted monopolization. Years later, Crandall settled with a slap on the wrist.

Frank Lorenzo had testified back in 1978 that deregulation would mean an attack on the labor movement, but he probably did not expect that he would be the attacker. In 1981, Lorenzo—flush with cash from his attempted takeover of National—tried to buy the much bigger Continental Airlines. The negotiations were heated, and Continental's chief, Al Feldman, committed suicide in his office in their midst. Lorenzo completed the merger the next year, and in 1983 took Continental into

bankruptcy. He shut the airline down completely and reopened
with about half the number of workers, who were now paid half
the salary. He put former Kennedy aide Phil Bakes in charge of
the airline. The episode turned Lorenzo into the most hated figure among airline employees.

Crandall also recognized that "deregulation is profoundly
anti-labor" and that it meant a "massive transfer of wealth from
airline employees to airline passengers." To compete with the
non-unionized airlines, Crandall pitched American's unions on
creating a system of A-scales and B-scales. Existing employees
would keep their jobs and salaries. But new employees would
start on a B-scale and be paid significantly less. The unions
accepted the deal, because it was the lesser of two evils. Unlike
their friends at Continental, at least they would keep their jobs
and salaries. Importantly, Crandall's approach meant that, as
American got bigger, it would not only gain further advantages
from its size, it would also see its average cost drop. United tried
to copy Crandall's strategy. But the airline failed to get an agreement with its unions and instead faced a massive strike.

By 1984, industry insiders had concluded that bigger was
better and smaller airlines would simply not be able to compete.
The fierce competitive battles continued—including battles
over who would buy the many ailing and failing airlines around
the country. United bought Pan Am's entire Pacific division,
becoming the biggest airline in the United States. Corporate
raider Carl Icahn entered the arena in 1985 with a proposal to
buy out TWA. With blood in the water, other sharks circled
TWA. Eastern Airlines, run by former astronaut Frank Borman,
made a run at it. Lorenzo started buying up shares because he
wanted TWA's CRS system for Texas Air's growing empire.

74   TWA was a house divided. Its management was worried that Icahn would sell the company for parts. TWA's unions hated Lorenzo so much that they were willing to take even bigger wage cuts for Icahn than TWA had wanted. Ironically, had they agreed to the original cuts, TWA might not have been as appealing a target. Icahn ultimately got the company, but Lorenzo was the real winner. As with his failed bid for National, he once again made a killing on the rising stock price.

Over at American Airlines, Crandall had finally perfected the yield management approach he had discovered nearly a decade earlier. He announced in 1985 that one in three seats would now be Super Saver fares, matching the rock-bottom prices of Don Burr's People Express. American's play would destroy People Express because American offered better service and a bigger network for the same price. Burr's response was to buy Frontier Airlines, thereby getting a CRS system, western routes and airport slots, and a frequent flyer program of his own. But the Frontier purchase ended up being a big mistake. The airline was in bad economic shape, and its culture clashed with Burr's no-frills company. Both United and Lorenzo made failed bids to take Frontier off Burr's hands, and Burr was forced to put Frontier in bankruptcy. At that point, Lorenzo reappeared. Seeing an opportunity to take control of Newark airport, he bought up People Express and Frontier. In less than a decade, Don Burr had come full circle. He was once again working for Frank Lorenzo.

Over and over, the mergers continued. Lorenzo added Eastern to his portfolio in 1986, and moved Bakes from Continental to run the troubled airline. Icahn and USAir both made plays for Piedmont (which had already bought Pacific Southwest and

Suburban Airlines). USAir won. TWA merged with Ozark, con-
solidating its fortress hub in St. Louis. Northwest and Republic.
Midway and Air Florida. Southwest and Muse. Jet America and
Alaska. American and AirCal. Delta and Western. It was a feed-
ing frenzy. Elizabeth Dole's Department of Transportation
approved merger after merger, in some cases over the objections of its own staff. Crandall later observed that more stringent antitrust enforcement would have made little difference.
"If you're going to have a deregulated industry, you're inevitably
going to have a small number of large carriers," he said. "If those
mergers had not been approved, I think it would have inevitably
led to the failures of the small carriers."

But mergers didn't necessarily mean that the now bigger
airlines were well run. Crandall's approach of slow growth and
expansion had made American profitable for every year that
decade. But Lorenzo's polyglot empire was in much worse shape.
Texas Air now included People Express, Frontier, New York Air,
Rocky Mountain Airways, Provincetown-Boston Airlines, Britt
Airways, Bar Harbor Airways, and Continental. When Bakes
arrived at Eastern, he found it in dire straits. Eastern had so little
cash it had even turned off the fountain in its courtyard to save
energy costs. Bakes told Eastern's employees in 1987 that the
airline needed $490 million per year in wage cuts. The pilots and
flight attendants had already agreed to 20 percent cuts as part of
the acquisition and didn't want more. The machinists' contract
wasn't up for a year, and they weren't likely to budge without a
fight. Eastern's situation was so bad that Lorenzo had to run the
airline separately rather than merge it with Continental.

But it is not clear whether that would have mattered.
Continental was itself a mess. The airline was scheduling crews

76 by hand. Its records were so disorganized that it couldn't give refunds within the legally mandated time frame, subjecting the airline to thousands of dollars in fines. Since People Express had encouraged passengers not to carry luggage, its ground crews had little experience with baggage handling. Continental was soon losing 500 to 1,000 bags per day, ten times the rate of other airlines. Almost half its flights were delayed. More broadly, airports everywhere were overloaded with flights, as big airlines moved toward hub-and-spokes models, but without necessary airport expansions to cover the additional volume. One Eastern pilot was so frustrated by tarmac delays in 1986 that he turned around before takeoff, re-parked at the terminal, and walked off the plane. Transportation Secretary Elizabeth Dole eventually gave the airlines antitrust immunity so they could coordinate their schedules. To prevent chaos in the industry, the government—at least with respect to scheduling—was authorizing a cartel.

The Great Debate
Southwest's longtime leader, Herb Kelleher, liked to say that the airline business was the "closest thing to war in peacetime." The story of the 1980s shows why. Competitors big and small battled fiercely for dominance—and for survival. But what do these battles suggest about the deregulatory experiment? Does warfare-by-other-means prove deregulation was a success—or a failure?

Answering this question is challenging for two reasons. First, we have to pick some criteria upon which to evaluate deregulation. Some people might want to focus on prices, others on the predictions of advocates, still others on the broader

goals that society has for air travel. Second, we have to figure out
when to evaluate airline deregulation. The industry has looked
different at different times—and it changed considerably in its
first decade. An observer trying to see if airline deregulation
"worked" would have a very different view of the matter in 1982
compared to 1989—or 2005.

In 1988, ten years after deregulation, two titans in the airline sector looked back over these battles and engaged in a
heated debate over whether deregulation was successful. One
was economist, former CAB chair, and deregulation advocate Alfred Kahn. The other was Melvin Brenner, who worked
for a decade in the federal government, including at the CAB,
before becoming an executive at American Airlines and TWA.
Both Kahn and Brenner recognized that airline deregulation had
not fully lived up to the claims the deregulators had made. As
Kahn admitted, even advocates for deregulation were deeply
surprised at the results along at least four lines: "1) the turbulence and painfulness of the process; 2) the reconcentration of
the industry; 3) the intensification of price discrimination and
monopolistic exploitation; and 4) the deterioration in quality of
airline service."

Using the Kahn-Brenner debate as an entry point, we can
evaluate whether airline deregulation succeeded along a variety
of metrics. What happened with competition and concentration? Industry dynamics and labor? Prices and quality of service? Geographic access? As we shall see, over and over again,
the advocates for deregulation were proven wrong.

78   **Competition and Concentration**
Immediately after deregulation there was a major burst of competition in the airline industry, followed in the years after by
waves of consolidation. With open entry into the airline industry, new entrants, including many low-cost, no-frills carriers,
began offering air service. By 1985, the market share of the ten
big airlines had dropped from 87 percent to 75 percent. But over
the next few years, more than 200 carriers either merged with
others or went out of business. By the end of the decade, the
nine biggest airlines had a 92 percent market share—higher
than before deregulation. Kahn acknowledged this reality:

> [O]ne of the most pleasant surprises of the early deregu-
> lation experience was the large-scale entry of new, highly
> competitive carriers, so probably the most unpleasant
> one has been the reversal of that trend—the departures
> of almost all of them, the reconcentration of the indus-
> try both nationally and at the major hubs, the diminish-
> ing disciplinary effectiveness of potential entry by totally
> new firms, and the increased likelihood, in consequence,
> of monopolistic exploitation.

A critical question, of course, was why. Why did the initial
burst of competition give way to consolidation?
Kahn identified a variety of reasons for this development.
First, bigger carriers were "developing and dominating hubs."
Dominance in hub airports made it difficult for rivals with fewer
flights to compete. Second, big carriers developed computer-
ized reservation systems (CRS) and frequent flyer programs.
Reservation systems enabled travel agents to search and easily

book flights across multiple carriers—but it disproportionally benefited the carriers that owned the CRS. American Airlines, for example, made sure that the first flight that popped up on its CRS was always an American flight.* Frequent flyer programs create benefits for travelers, but they also strengthen carrier loyalty and dissuade passengers from switching airlines. That reduces competition too—and benefits airlines that fly to more places. Third, big carriers discovered they could discount their fares to levels that smaller competitors couldn't match. This meant they could win fare wars because they could outlast their rivals. Weaker airlines were thus likely to get eaten by bigger firms via merger. To this list, Brenner added that many non-scheduled, low-price charter airlines had reduced service or gone out of business after deregulation.

Brenner and other critics were quick to point out that the advocates of deregulation were wrong about open entry leading to competition. The Chicago School and its allies embraced what was later called the "theory of contestable markets." The idea was that in most sectors, there were "no effective barriers

* The biggest airlines in the 1960s and 1970s first adopted CRS, and travel agents were able to book flights through these platforms. Airlines that didn't create their own CRS had to pay to have their flights included. American Airlines engaged in self-preferencing on its CRS. American knew that the first flight that came up in a search was most likely to be picked, so it ensured that American would win the first line in its CRS; it also demoted its competitors. In addition, American collected data on sales from its competitors through its CRS. Congress asked the CAB to investigate whether the airlines that owned CRS were preferencing their own flights over competitors. Before the CAB's dissolution in 1985, it issued nondiscrimination rules barring self-preferencing in CRS. Ultimately, airlines divested their CRS business lines. With CRS now separated from the airlines, the Department of Transportation, in 2004, allowed the nondiscrimination rules to sunset.

80   to entry, and therefore there would always be a sufficient threat
of new competition to keep incumbent carriers from abusing a
monopoly position." But the airline industry did, in fact, have
serious barriers to entry: there are limited numbers of airports,
gates, and runways. One can't just fly between two places—
there has to be somewhere to land. And network effects mean
that airlines are more desirable if they can offer more routes.
Both of these things make it harder for new entrants to compete.
Indeed, it was regulation that had allowed relatively smaller carriers to operate successfully before 1978 because, as Brenner put
it, regulation had "neutralized size as a market factor."

A related lesson of the 1980s was that the airline industry had economies of scale, despite the claims of deregulation
advocates a decade before. Economies of scale exist when there
are increasing benefits (or lower costs) as a business scales up in
size. Kahn acknowledged the mistake forthrightly: "We advocates of deregulation were misled by the apparent lack of evidence of economies of scale." He further noted that he and
others "did not anticipate the thoroughgoing movement to
hub-and-spoke operations and the dominant role it would
play in determining the balance of competitive advantage and
disadvantage."

Network effects and economies of scale made size valuable
on both the passenger side (demand) and the airline side (supply). On the demand side, passengers are more willing to fly with
a carrier that has a large network because they can fly to more
destinations, with fewer switches between airlines (what are
called "interline" changes). This makes perfect sense. It's better to fly from New York to Des Moines on the same airline, even
if you have to make a connection, than to book two different

tickets on two different airlines. More cities and routes make an airline more desirable. This is also true for the number of flights. For both airports and routes, airlines that have greater frequency increase their market share disproportionately. On the supply side, large airlines can spread their costs more broadly over more routes. Scale therefore offers some financial security to withstand fierce price competition on some routes.

Importantly, these features mean that airlines have an incentive to shift from point-to-point service to a hub-and-spokes model. Every city that connects into a hub enables the people from that city to connect to *every other destination* the hub serves. As a result, the benefits from each additional spoke are much greater than simply one additional route. If Delta goes from your city to Atlanta, you don't just get access to one city, but to hundreds of locations, with only one connection. Predictably, airlines increasingly concentrated their operations in regional hubs. When an airline reaches an extreme market share of a single airport, it is referred to as having a "fortress hub," a position of power that makes it hard for other competitors to get a foothold in that city. Ten years after deregulation, concentration had increased at airports across the country.

Kahn "lament[ed]" the increased concentration in the industry, but he thought it was "absurd" to blame deregulation. Rather, he argued that the fault lay with the Department of Transportation, which had allowed mergers to take place over the same period. But Kahn made two errors in this conclusion. The first was the point about network effects and economies of scale. The fact that they existed made it inevitable that the industry would eventually consolidate after deregulation. Second, Kahn ignored the fact that antitrust law was

FIGURE 1

Single Carrier Concentration at Major Airports Pre- and Post-Deregulation

AIRPORT		1977		1987
Baltimore/Washington	24.5%	US Air	60.0%	US Air*
Cincinnati	35.0%	Delta	67.6%	Delta
Detroit Metropolitan	21.2%	Delta	64.9%	Northwest
Houston Intercontinental	20.4%	Continental	71.5%	Continental
Memphis	40.2%	Delta	86.7%	Northwest
Minneapolis/St. Paul	45.9%	Northwest	81.6%	Northwest
Nashville Metropolitan	28.2%	US Air	60.2%	American
Pittsburgh	43.7%	US Air	82.8%	US Air
St. Louis Lambert	39.1%	TWA	82.3%	TWA
Salt Lake City	39.6%	Western	74.5%	Delta

*includes Piedmont

Source: Andrew R. Goetz and Paul Stephen Dempsey, "Airline Deregulation Ten Years After: Something Foul in the Air." 54 J. Air L. & Com. 927, 941 (1989).

itself caught up in the same revolutionary policy change that Kahn had brought to airlines. In 1978, Robert Bork, a law professor associated with the Chicago School (and later a federal judge and failed nominee to the Supreme Court), published *The Antitrust Paradox.* The book was transformative in the field of antitrust law. Bork and the Chicago School's approach to antitrust was market friendly and focused on efficiency and lowering consumer prices, even if that meant allowing more mergers and consolidation. Bork's antitrust revolution stemmed from the same intellectual sources as Kahn's new thinking about deregulation. In light of that overlap, it is unclear why Kahn expected the Reagan administration to engage in aggressive antitrust enforcement. Indeed, Chicago School scholars pushed the Reagan administration to "prune" antitrust law as a way to further a deregulatory agenda.

Industry Dynamics

Advocates also thought deregulation would increase air traffic, passenger numbers, and load factors (how full the flight is). At first, the raw data showed an increase in air travel in the years after deregulation, and for decades, people would point to the expansion and growth of the industry as a great success story. But passenger volume was increasing before deregulation too. Between 1962 and 1967, for example, passenger volume doubled, and it nearly doubled again by 1978 despite slower growth around 1970. Looking at how the industry actually works—not just at surface-level data—the results were even less clear. The former airline executive Brenner argued that while the traffic *numbers* were up, the *rates* were not. In the 1970–1978 period, the growth rate in air traffic averaged 7.0 percent. But in the eight years after deregulation, traffic only increased by an average of 6.2 percent. The load factor data required similar care to understand from the perspective of the airline business. While the load factor itself had jumped from 54 percent to 60 percent after deregulation, meaning flights were now 60 percent full on average, the *break-even* load factor—how full flights had to be in order for the airline to break even—had increased from 53 percent to 62 percent. What this meant was that airlines had gone from above water by 1 percent to underwater by 2 percent. Even though there were fuller flights, airlines weren't breaking even.

By the late 1980s, the industry was in trouble. Financial losses were significant. "I doubt that most of us were fully prepared," Kahn said in 1988, "for the explosion of entry, massive restructurings of routes, price wars, labor-management conflict, bankruptcies and consolidations, and the generally dismal profit record of the last ten years." Kahn explained away financial

84   losses in the early 1980s as a function of the economic reces-
sion, higher fuel prices, and the air traffic controllers strike, but
by 1988 admitted that the losses in the later 1980s were a function of competition and, as a result, deregulation.

Labor
One of the benefits of the regulated system was to ensure stable industry dynamics for workers. Pilots, flight attendants,
baggage handlers, and other airline industry employees didn't
have to worry much about airlines going bankrupt and losing their jobs. Airline revenues were guaranteed because they
were an essential service for the country. Deregulation initially
unleashed competition, and with it, pressure to lower costs—
and that meant pressure to lower wages and benefits for workers. New, low-cost carriers, such as New York Air and People
Express, got into the airline business after deregulation, and
they didn't have unionized employees. This meant they could
offer lower wages compared to the legacy carriers. The legacy
carriers responded by pushing their unions to lower wages—
sometimes asking for wage cuts of 20 percent. American
Airlines created a B-scale with significantly lower wages for new
employees. When mergers took place, the new ownership often
pushed unions again to agree to lower wages. Flight attendants,
pilots, and machinist unions were thus often at odds with airline management, leading to strikes.

The effects on workers and increasing labor unrest in the
airline industry caused serious pain for workers—and politicians heard about it. Even Senator Ted Kennedy, one of
the champions of deregulation, seems to have had second
thoughts. At a 1988 event in Washington, Phil Bakes bumped

into Kennedy. Upon seeing Bakes, Kennedy boomed, "This goddamn dereg . . . you know, Phil, you double-crossed me. You lied
to me. You said the unions were going to support deregulation."
People at the event gawked as Kennedy continued to shout at
Bakes about airline deregulation.

For his part, Kahn did not care much about employee wages.
He thought reductions in worker wages were "an additional,
substantial benefit." "[M]onopoly wages," he said, "are no more
acceptable than monopoly profits." Even if the conflicts between
labor and management harmed the quality and safety of service,
Kahn thought they were simply "part of the price we are usually
willing to pay for the benefits of a competitive economy."

Prices

The most celebrated claim of advocates for airline deregulation
is that prices would go down. Before digging into the evidence,
it is worth noting that under the theory of deregulation prices
should go down. With deregulation, we should expect airlines
to abandon some expensive routes to focus on cheaper, bus-
ier ones (meaning lower prices across the board) and that more
competition on the busy routes would mean fare wars, further
lowering prices. If prices therefore did not go down—or did not
go down far more quickly than under regulation—that would be
a devastating indictment of deregulation indeed.

Initially, prices on many routes did fall, due to increased
competition from low-cost carriers. In his retrospective, Kahn
argued that price competition had largely been a success: prices
were down between 1976 and 1986, and more passengers traveled on discount tickets. But the data were not so clear. Brenner's
view was that "[t]he widespread impression is that deregulation

86   has led to sharply reduced fares . . . is incorrect." Looking indus-
      trywide and comparing pre-deregulation trends, Brenner
      showed that while there were significant price declines by 1984,
      these declines were primarily the result of service from low-cost
      carrier People Express offering rock-bottom prices. People
      Express, however, had since become a casualty of consolidation
      and merged into Continental Airlines. As a result, by 1987, the
      price benefits stemming from deregulation had diminished.

      It also isn't enough to look at prices after deregulation;
      it matters what they looked like before deregulation too. One
      commonly used, standardized metric in the airline industry
      is "yield per passenger mile," which is the amount the indus-
      try earns on a per mile basis. Adjusted for inflation, Brenner
      found that yield had "declined by an average of 2.6 percent per
      year in the eight deregulated years between 1978 and 1986. This
      was not materially different than the average decline of 2.2 per-
      cent per year over the same period prior to deregulation." The
      post-deregulation numbers were also on the optimistic side
      for two reasons. First, the 1986 data included the lower fares
      prompted by People Express, which no longer existed.* The sec-
      ond problem was that post-deregulation air transportation

      * In response, Kahn argued for taking a pre-deregulation baseline of 1970–
      1976 because deregulatory efforts began prior to the passage of the 1978
      legislation, and he argued that this, in turn, showed much greater price
      benefits. Brenner responded that pre-1978 changes were possible under the
      statute, which means that total legislative deregulation was unnecessary
      to accomplish them. If the debate was about whether *legislative* reforms
      were successful, the 1978 date was more appropriate. This point is critically
      important because it placed Kahn in a bind: either his actions from 1977–
      1978 were permissible under airline regulation, thus rendering legislative
      deregulation unnecessary, or they were impermissible, rendering his actions
      illegal, but legislative deregulation necessary.

involved more flight connections through hubs, so passengers
traveled more miles to get to the same destination. To simplify,
think about it this way: assume that a 100-mile flight between
two cities before deregulation costs the airline $100 and yields
the same amount in revenue. That would mean a $1 per mile rev-
enue. After deregulation, you have to connect through a hub,
increasing the distance flown to 200 miles for the same trip.
If the price of the flight *went up* to $150, the revenue per mile
would only be $0.75. It appears that prices have gone down, even
though a passenger is paying more and taking a less convenient
route.

Moreover, Brenner showed a steady decline in fares per
mile that began well *before* deregulation. Kahn argued that
this pre-deregulation decline was due to technological innovations. But there was no reason to think that had regulation remained—with fierce competition over service, rather

FIGURE 2
Fare per Mile, in Constant 1967 Dollars

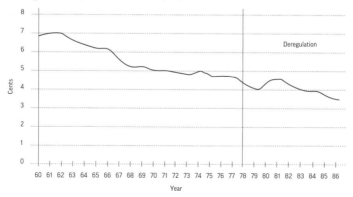

Source: From Brennan, *Rejoinder*.

88   than price—technological innovations might not also have
      continued.

      The question of declining overall fares has remained
controversial, with advocates claiming that prices fell after
deregulation—and often downplaying that they were falling before deregulation as well. In perhaps the most astonishing example, the Government Accountability Office issued a
report in 2006 with the striking title "Reregulating the Airline
Industry Would Likely Reverse Consumer Benefits and Not
Save Airline Pensions." The GAO offered seventeen different charts and graphs analyzing the airline industry. The first
four, covering aspects of industry growth, showed data before
and after deregulation. Twelve—including the charts on price
and competition—started at deregulation. The report then
acknowledges scholars who had argued that prices were in
decline prior to deregulation. But it barely responds to or ana-
lyzes this data. The report briefly notes that there was a steady
decline pre-deregulation and no sharp change when deregulation happened. It offers a chart showing as much, and then simply moves to the next section—without any further reflection
on the importance of the data.*

      Even with debates on average price levels, both advocates
and critics of deregulation agreed on one thing: prices had not
gone down uniformly. Instead, as Kahn put it,

---

* The GAO's comment on the broader view of price declines is surprising,
given the report's otherwise celebratory tone: "In fact, real average fares paid
per mile (yields) since 1962 do show a steady decline, reflecting both CAB
fare setting flexibility and cost-savings following the introduction of jet
service in the early 1960s, but without a sharp break in 1978 following the
deregulation of the industry."

FIGURE 3
Real Yield Trends, 1950–2004

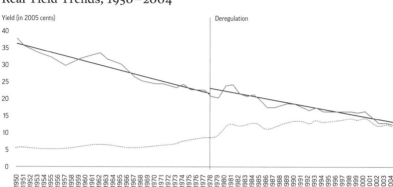

Source: From GAO analysis of Air Transport Association data.

That fares in the denser markets have gone down, dramatically, is unquestionable; that they have failed to go down as much in the thinner markets, or that unrestricted coach fares have actually increased (even in real terms) is likewise unquestionable.

Some routes were now "tremendous bargains," but others had "very steep price inflation." Comparing 1978 and 1987, a traveler leaving Detroit would pay 12 percent more to Los Angeles; 46 percent more to Salt Lake City; 136 percent more to Dallas; and 220 percent more to St. Louis. The source of these disparities was how much competition there was on these routes. Markets with more competition faced lower prices than those with less competition. The result was that "some parts of the public get bargains, while other passengers are subsidizing

90   those bargains by the steep escalation in their fares." Kahn
      largely conceded the point about geographic price differences.
      But he saw this as a positive development because the new
      prices reflected different costs.

      A bigger debate emerged over whether large carriers could
      undercut smaller ones. Kahn admitted that he "should have
      recognized . . . the naturally monopolistic or oligopolistic char-
      acter of most airline markets," but thought it was "extremely
      dubious" that some prices went up because others had declined
      due to fierce competition. In other words, he opposed the idea
      that there was a reverse cross-subsidy at work, by which those
      traveling along uncompetitive routes were subsidizing those on
      hotly competitive ones.

      Brenner, the former airline executive, responded that
      deregulation advocates had ignored the structure of costs
      for an airline. Most costs for airlines—ground crew, planes,
      maintenance—are fixed regardless of how many passengers
      take a flight. As a result, it was in the interest of a big carrier to
      match the lower fares of new, low-cost airlines and gain what-
      ever revenue it could. Even if the gains were not enough to
      cover its costs, that would be better than running the flight and
      earning zero revenue from an empty seat. Airlines would there-
      fore drop prices, including below the cost of service, simply to
      mitigate losses in a competitive environment.* When coupled

      ---

      * As another scholar notes, "[A]irlines sell a product which is instantly
      perishable. Once a scheduled flight closes its door and pulls away from the
      jetway, any empty seats are lost forever. They cannot be warehoused and
      sold another day, as can manufactured goods. It is as if a grocer were selling
      groceries which had the spoilage properties of open jars of unrefrigerated
      mayonnaise. He would be forced to have a fire sale every afternoon, for any
      unsold inventory would have to be discarded."

with the other advantages of big carriers—higher quality service, more frequent flights, a larger network—the low-cost,
small-network, limited-frequency, no-frills airline had no
chance of winning a head-to-head battle. It would not be able
to get the volume needed to make its low costs work because
the big carrier would match it on price. This was precisely the
strategy that Crandall adopted at American.

Quality of Service

After deregulation, the quality of airline service clearly declined.
Surveys of travelers surfaced a long list of complaints: "late
departures, crowded seating, long lines at check-in, unap-
petizing food, overbooked aircraft, and an unacceptably long
wait for baggage." There were allegations that competition and
cost-savings had led airlines to defer aircraft maintenance. The
Department of Transportation, for example, found that, in the
first six years of deregulation, resources going to aircraft maintenance dropped 30 percent. Nearly half of pilots believed that
their companies delayed maintenance for too long.

Another increasingly important issue was congestion.
Deregulating entry meant increased traffic and shifts in traffic
patterns, and airport capacity had not adapted quickly enough.
In particular, the shift to hub-and-spokes systems put extra
pressure on airports by concentrating flight arrivals and departures. In Atlanta, for example, there were only five hours per day
with more than fifty arrivals in 1978. By 1987, every hour from
7:00 a.m. to 11:00 p.m. had more than fifty flights. This kind
of pressure, of course, meant that any flight delays would have
a cascading effect across the airline's schedule. TWA's hub in
St. Louis was either an origin, destination, or connection for

79 percent of the airline's flights in 1987. One city with airport delays could have a "systemwide chain reaction" on the whole airline nationally.

Kahn admitted his failures here too. He and other deregulation advocates "did not foresee the deterioration in the average quality of the flying experience, and in particular the congestion and delays that have plagued air travelers in recent years." But he argued that these factors were not a "legitimate" consideration. In fact, "these discomforts are a sign of the success of deregulation, not its failure." They merely showed that travelers preferred lower fares coupled with worse service. The argument was a weird one, but it is repeated frequently, even today. Despite admitting that he misunderstood the dynamics of the airline business, he still seemed to believe that the market worked just fine—and that passengers preferred lower prices over better service. It didn't seem to cross his mind that consumer choices couldn't fix these problems because of the dynamics of the industry.

Geographic Access

One of the central fears of airline deregulation was that smaller communities would lose airline service. The Airline Deregulation Act even included subsidies to smaller communities as a guard against the possibility that that would happen. Kahn declared unequivocal victory on this point. "Thanks partly to the Essential Air Services Program incorporated in the 1978 Act," he wrote, "not a single community that enjoyed a minimum level of certificated service at the time of deregulation has lost it."

But members of Congress that represented rural areas and smaller cities saw it differently. Many of them swiftly changed their minds about airline deregulation. As early as 1985, Tennessee senator Jim Sasser, who had voted for deregulation and then observed how it had hurt east Tennessee, said that deregulation was no longer in favor "in the Congress as House members and Senators see the air service into their [s]tates declining precipitously." The following year, Senator Robert Byrd of West Virginia was unequivocal:

> [T]his is one Senator who regrets that he voted for airline deregulation. It has penalized States like West Virginia, where many of the airlines pulled out quickly following deregulation and the prices zoomed into the stratosphere—doubled, tripled and, in some instances, quadrupled. So we have poorer air service and much more costly air service than we in West Virginia had prior to deregulation. I admit my error; I confess my unwisdom, and I am truly sorry for having voted for deregulation.
>
> I would welcome the opportunity to vote for reregulation because we people in the rural States are paying the bill.

In addition to reductions in service and higher prices, smaller cities had fewer nonstop flights. Airlines served 5,832 markets nonstop in 1978 but had dropped 3,286 by 1983. True, some smaller communities were better off even without nonstop service because they had access to more places via major hubs. But they also now faced higher prices. Second, the loss of nonstop

94   service to small communities and the rise of hubs were problem-
      atic from a broader economic perspective. As Brenner put it,

> [T]ransportation is a basic part of the economic/social/
> cultural infrastructure, which affects the efficiency of all
> other business activities in a community and the quality
> of life of its residents. The ability of a city to retain exist-
> ing industries, and attract new ones, is uniquely depen-
> dent upon the adequacy, convenience, and reasonable
> pricing of its airline service.

Concentration meant increases in economic growth for the
winners—cities with major hubs—and trouble for those who
had more limited service. The network effects and concentration unleashed by deregulation would thus have an indirect
effect on the economic fates of entire cities and regions.

Conclusions

The participants in the great debate over airline deregulation
at the end of the 1980s came to different conclusions—about
deregulation in 1978, the success of the experiment, and the
possibilities for the future. Kahn thought the downsides of
deregulation were a price worth paying for competition.

> As I have pointed out for decades (with a total lack of orig-
> inality), any society that craves stability and predictability
> will opt for regulation and insulation from competition;
> a society that is willing to pay the price of instability in
> order to encourage creativity, innovation, and continuous
> improvement in productivity will opt for competition.

Kahn also thought there was little value in attempting incremental reforms to address the downsides of the deregulated system: "'[P]artial re-regulation' is, I suggest, just about as feasible as partial pregnancy."

Brenner, on the other hand, looked back at 1978 from a critical perspective. He observed that deregulation was premised on the "rejection of the oligopoly scenario," and that "[i]t is inconceivable that Congress would have enacted deregulation if it foresaw that the public would end up with neither the protection of regulation nor the protection of wide-open multi-carrier competition." Instead, a decade of experience showed that the airline industry had "special characteristics," and that it was better suited to a "partial 'public utility' approach."

Importantly, Brenner also observed that there were ideological factors at work. Advocates had embraced a free-market theory that rejected out of hand the goals and benefits of the American tradition of regulated capitalism. Admitting that deregulation did not live up to its promises was essential to prevent making the same mistakes in the future or in other areas of economic life. Still, Brenner did not argue for returning to full-on regulation. He hoped for a middle ground. If something wasn't done, airlines would continue as an unregulated oligopoly—something no one had wanted or thought was desirable. The consequences of that regime would be disastrous for the industry and for the public.

Airlines Unleashed

The American tradition of regulated capitalism ensured that critically important industries would be stable and effective—and wouldn't become predatory. But after the Airline Deregulation Act, airlines were let loose into the world of unregulated capitalism. On the one hand, many aspects of the industry continued successfully. The number of flights and passengers continued to increase. And safety did not precipitously decline.

But as the opponents of deregulation predicted, the industry has become more chaotic. From 1938 to 1978, the industry was relatively stable. But after deregulation, it became subject to boom-and-bust cycles. Profits were in the stratosphere in the late 1990s and the 2010s. But when passenger demand plummeted in response to the Gulf War, September 11, and COVID-19, the industry went into free fall, leading to bankruptcies, government bailouts and support, and further mergers and consolidation.

Airlines have also responded to unregulated capitalism in
predictable ways. The big carriers have done everything they can
to gain monopoly power—they've waged predatory price wars
to force out competitors, established fortress hubs at big airports, and abandoned unprofitable cities. Airlines now charge
extra for more leg room, checked bags, and snacks. They've also
learned from Wall Street that finance can be more profitable
than industry. Airlines now operate like banks, creating their
own currency via their frequent flyer and credit card programs.
In the age of deregulation, airlines are unleashed.

Crises and Consolidation
By the late 1980s and early 1990s, airlines were in a dangerous
situation. The large and expansive United Airlines was growing
vertically, with the acquisitions of Hertz, Westin, and Hilton—
all part of Dick Ferris's plan to integrate all aspects of travel.
But Frank Lorenzo's price wars kept airfares low—and earnings too. With a stock price trading below the company's true
value, UAL, United's parent, was an attractive target for arbitrage or takeover. In 1987, Donald Trump bought 5 percent of
UAL. Ferris diluted the stock with more shares, and United's
unions attempted to buy the airline. With the price up, Trump
cashed out and walked away. By 1989, United was also the target of a leveraged buyout (LBO), an acquisition of a company
using borrowed money. United's management, pilots union,
non-union workers, and British Airways all joined together to
make a deal to stop the LBO. That same year, Trump proposed
to buy American, offering nearly $40 more per share than its
stock price. American's stock surged. But President George

98 H. W. Bush's transportation secretary, Samuel Skinner, was worried about foreign ownership and excessive debt in airlines. When he said so, there was a huge sell-off in airline stocks. The United deal fell apart, and Trump dropped his bid for American. Lorenzo's empire was in an even worse position. Eastern's unions went on strike in 1989, and Lorenzo took the airline into bankruptcy. After that, Lorenzo decided that he was part of the problem at Texas Air, and he stepped aside so the company could move beyond him.

Then came the Gulf War, which raised fuel costs and created fears of terrorism. Coupled with a weak economy, air travel plummeted. At the time, the industry was already financially vulnerable. Consolidation in the late 1980s, coupled with leveraged buyouts, had left some airlines with high debt-to-capital ratios. Continental didn't have the cash to withstand the downturn and filed for bankruptcy again, the second time in less than a decade. Pan Am went bankrupt in 1991, having sold off its valuable international routes year after year in a desperate need for cash. Eastern went into liquidation. Midway into bankruptcy, then liquidation. America West into bankruptcy. In 1990 and 1991, airlines lost $6 billion, more than all the profits they had made since the 1920s combined.

With the big carriers still under strain, competition reemerged in the early 1990s after the war. New airlines like ValuJet/AirTran, Spirit, Frontier, and Kiwi started operations, and some smaller, older carriers like Southwest saw rising growth. Fares continued to decline over this time period—though, as in the 1980s, prices were higher in smaller markets and in markets with less competition.

The new unregulated environment also brought cutthroat price competition between the big carriers and low-cost
entrants. The rationale was clearly stated by deregulatory advocate Michael Levine, who later served as president of Lorenzo's
New York Air:

> Match, or better yet beat, the new entrant's lowest fare
> with a low fare restricted to confine its attractiveness to
> the leisure-oriented, price-sensitive sector of the market.
> Match business-oriented fares and offer extra benefits
> to retain the loyalties of travel agents and frequent fly-
> ers. Add frequency where possible, to "sandwich" the new
> entrant's departures between one's own departures. Make
> sure enough seats are available on your flights in the mar-
> ket to accommodate increases in traffic caused by the fare
> war. In short, leave no traveler with either a price or sched-
> ule incentive to fly the new entrant.
>
> The incumbent will not operate profitably under
> such conditions, especially if, as is usually the case, it is
> a higher-cost airline than its competitor. Its losses will,
> however, be cushioned by the hub traffic not subject to the
> new entrant's price competition, and its information and
> principal-agent advantages will tend to keep passengers as
> long as there is price parity.

In the 1990s, the big airlines seemed to adopt exactly this
approach. When low-cost carrier Vanguard Airlines began
operating between Kansas City (MCI) and Dallas-Fort Worth
(DFW) in 1995, American (which had and still has a hub at DFW)

matched Vanguard's fares, ultimately pushing the low-cost competitor out by the end of the year. With Vanguard out of the market, American "immediately began reducing its service and raising its fares . . . up to 80 percent higher than when Vanguard was in the market." The short-term downsides of running low- or no-profit flights were a strategy to crush competitors. As Crandall said, "If you are not going to get them out[,] then no point to diminish profit."

The Clinton administration attempted to go after pred-atory pricing and other anticompetitive practices. In 1998, it issued guidelines to spur competition at large airports, only to face pushback from airlines who claimed this was the first step down a slippery slope to re-regulation. When those efforts were scuttled, the Justice Department brought a law-suit against American Airlines. The Justice Department argued that American tried to push low-cost airlines like Vanguard, Western Pacific, and Sun Jet out of the market. The 1999 case was the first airline predatory pricing case since deregulation. But in the new era of weak antitrust enforcement, the fed-eral district court found for American: "There is no doubt that American may be a difficult, vigorous, even brutal competitor," the court said. "But here, it engaged only in bare, but not brass, knuckle competition."

September 11 caused a second crisis for the industry. The shock to demand was immediate—the grounding of all flights for four days, followed by new security rules, the wars in Afghanistan and Iraq, and higher fuel prices. With demand down, the industry lost almost $35 billion between 2001 and 2005. United, Delta, Northwest, and US Airways (twice) filed for bankruptcy. TWA—one of the oldest airlines in the

country—was acquired by American in 2001. Some of the biggest airlines in the country had their pension plans bailed out by
the federal Pension Benefit Guaranty Corporation (PBGC).

In response to 9/11, Congress swiftly passed the Air
Transportation Safety and System Stabilization Act (ATSSSA),
which was an industry bailout. The ATSSSA provided $5 bil-
lion in compensation to airlines for the stoppage of flights and
expected future losses. It also created an Air Transportation
Stabilization Board (ATSB), which was empowered to give up to
$10 billion in loans and loan guarantees to the airlines. The fed-
eral government began to subsidize airline insurance and it created a federally subsidized terrorism risk insurance program.

America West, the eighth largest airline in the country,
which had filed for bankruptcy after the Gulf War, was the first
to apply to the ATSB in the fall of 2001. US Airways, United, and
a number of small airlines had filed with the ATSB by the sum-
mer of 2002, with United pilots even agreeing to a pay cut if the
airline would seek federal assistance. The ATSB approved the
US Airways application swiftly and ultimately rejected those of
United and some smaller airlines.

By the late 2000s, another wave of consolidation was
underway. Aloha Airlines, ATA, and Skybus ended service, and
Frontier went into bankruptcy. Delta and Northwest merged in
2008, as did Southwest and ATA. United and Continental established an alliance that year, which became a merger in 2010.
Frontier and Midwest merged in 2009. Southwest and AirTran
in 2010. American and US Airways in 2013. In a notable 2008
speech amid the churn in the industry, now former American
Airlines CEO Bob Crandall reiterated his objections to deregulation of the industry. He noted that the US airlines were

102 "laggards in every category, including fleet age, service quality, and international reputation." He observed that "unfettered
competition just doesn't work very well in certain industries."
And he concluded that "it is time to acknowledge that airlines
look and are more like utilities than ordinary businesses."

At the same time, global airline alliances—like SkyTeam,
Oneworld, and Star Alliance—had emerged. Airline alliances
are another form of consolidation: a partnership between global
airlines that allows passengers to fly through a single network. By the late 2010s, Star Alliance had 100 percent market
share between Frankfurt, Germany, and Newark, Washington,
Chicago, Los Angeles, and San Francisco. SkyTeam had 100
percent market share between Amsterdam and New York-JFK,
Los Angeles, Detroit, Atlanta, and Minneapolis. Oneworld had
100 percent market share between Madrid and Chicago, Los
Angeles, and Philadelphia.

The 2010s were the most profitable decade for airlines
in history. They were also an era of consolidation in another,
far more subtle, fashion. Recall that the American tradition of regulated capitalism was sharply opposed to horizontal and vertical relationships in network, platform, and utility
businesses. In the airline industry, the law had long prohibited cross-ownership within "any phase of aeronautics." The
Airmail Act of 1934 banned horizontal shareholding, interlocking directorates, and conglomeration more broadly. These
provisions survived the changes of the 1930s and were critical
components of the Civil Aeronautics Act of 1938. But with the
demise of regulated capitalism, they were weakened in the 1978
Airline Deregulation Act and ultimately repealed by the Civil
Aeronautics Board Sunset Act of 1984.

By the 2010s, airlines were increasingly subject to horizontal shareholding. That is, shareholders owned stock in multiple, rival airlines. Seven shareholders together had 60 percent ownership of United Airlines between 2013 and 2015. But they also owned 27.5 percent of Delta, 27.3 percent of JetBlue, and 23.3 percent of Southwest. Economic research has shown that horizontal shareholding means higher prices—some 3 to 10 percent in the case of airlines. As Harvard Law School professor Einer Elhauge explains, "[T]he reason is that firms maximize profits by competing only when the profits from taking market share away from other firms exceed the interest in keeping marketwide prices high." For the airlines, it's better to keep market prices high, rather than competing with each other. Importantly, keeping industry profits high does not require communication or explicit collusion. Airline CEOs no longer feel the need, as Crandall did, to propose jointly raising prices. It is in their shareholders' interest—and therefore theirs—to keep prices high. To the extent the airline industry was already an oligopoly, it is now further concentrated through these "common owners."

The third major crisis was the demand shock associated with the COVID-19 pandemic, which prompted a severe decline in passenger air travel. As we have seen, commentators and critics observed that the airlines once again needed federal support after years of extreme profitability. This time, the reason the airlines did not have a rainy day fund was because they had spent "96 percent of their cash profits on stock buybacks to enrich investors and their own executives." Delta, for example, had just finished its most profitable decade ever. The CARES Act, passed in March 2020, provided $50 billion in funding for the airlines, on the condition that they not reduce pay or benefits to employees. But airlines scuttled the spirit of the law by pushing early retirement packages.

The pandemic proved that the airline industry is not healthy, stable, or resilient. For an industry that was consistently profitable before deregulation, the years since have been highly variable. In nearly one-third of the years since deregulation, airlines have faced losses.

TABLE 1

US Passenger Airlines Profit and Loss, 1978–2021, Data from Airlines for America

1978	Profit	1993	Profit	2008	Loss
1979	Profit	1994	Profit	2009	Profit
1980	Loss	1995	Profit	2010	Profit
1981	Loss	1996	Profit	2011	Profit
1982	Loss	1997	Profit	2012	Profit
1983	Profit	1998	Profit	2013	Profit
1984	Profit	1999	Profit	2014	Profit
1985	Profit	2000	Profit	2015	Profit
1986	Profit	2001	Loss	2016	Profit
1987	Profit	2002	Loss	2017	Profit
1988	Profit	2003	Loss	2018	Profit
1989	Profit	2004	Loss	2019	Profit
1990	Loss	2005	Loss	2020	Loss
1991	Loss	2006	Profit	2021	Loss
1992	Loss	2007	Profit		

In some ways, the airlines have become like the "too big to fail" Wall Street banks. They have had extremely profitable periods, followed by crises, and then government support. Airlines are simply too important to the economy and our society to let them collapse. But the drawback, as with other "too big to fail" industries, is that private shareholders get all the upside in the profitable years, and taxpayers are faced with the downsides of bailouts and support in the crisis years.

Airlines as Banks

Airlines are like banks in another way too. Since the 1980s, there has been spectacular growth in frequent flyer programs. But frequent flyer programs are no longer like a punch-card at the local sandwich shop, where your eleventh sandwich is free. Three changes, over three decades, have transformed this system. Starting in 1987, major airlines began collaborating with credit cards. Airlines realized that joining with a bank to create a branded credit card would increase spending, and that it was more lucrative to sell points to the banks than to other partners like rental car companies or hotels (more on this in a moment). In the 1990s, airlines started expanding the number of fare categories. With increasingly complex fare structures, Virgin America realized that the amount people spent was far more important than mileage flown. In 2007, it therefore adopted a revenue-based model for its loyalty program. This meant that earning points would be a function of dollars spent, not miles flown. These shifts fundamentally transformed the industry.

Here's how the system works now. Airlines create frequent flyer points out of thin air, and then sell them to banks at (usually) between 1 and 1.5 cents a point. The airlines make money on these sales. When individuals use their credit card, the bank (which is co-branded with the airline on the card) awards points to the individual for spending on certain items or services. The banks and credit card companies make money on swipe fees when the card is used. Points systems are a perk that induces and then keeps customers using their card instead of a competitor card.

On the other side of the ledger, individuals accruing points in their account can use those points to pay for flights or other products and services. Importantly, there's no cost to the airline until the points are redeemed. The points in the account represent money the airline has gotten for nothing—it created them and sold them to the bank. One key question, of course, is what the exchange rates are for this currency: How much does it cost partners to buy points, and how many points does it cost individuals to buy goods and services? Airlines set these terms, and some, like United, have recently removed some of their award charts, making rates opaque.

In 2020, when airlines were seeking support during the COVID-19 pandemic, appraisers valued American Airlines' AAdvantage program at between $19.5 and $31.5 billion. United's MileagePlus was valued at $21.9 billion. In comparison, the stock market values those airlines at merely $5 to $10 billion. Loyalty programs are worth so much because they have turned airlines into financial institutions. Airline points are a currency, and the airline is the monetary authority—like the Federal Reserve. The difference between the Fed and an airline is that airlines also control which goods and services its currency can purchase. So important are these programs that, in 2022, American Airlines eliminated the legacy approach to valuing

miles flown separately from non-flight dollars spent. It now
treats ordinary credit card spending the same as miles flown for
purposes of accruing points.

As a result of these developments, some commentators
have observed that airlines are now basically banks that just
happen, incidentally, to operate airlines. In addition to operating an unregulated currency, airlines' incentives may be to facilitate their points programs even over their air services. Points
programs also show how fragile the airline business is. The
unregulated environment is so fierce that it has pushed airlines
into credit card partnerships where profits are more reliable.

Geographic Inequality Revisited

As critics of deregulation predicted, airlines reduced flights to
some cities, withdrew from smaller hubs as they consolidated
into bigger fortress hubs, and dropped some cities altogether.
Kansas City, for example, was a hub for TWA, and then lost that
hub, only to become a hub to Eastern, which then went out of
business. Fares also started varying considerably by region.
Starting in the 1990s, fares were higher in the Southeast than
other regions, largely because of cities' reliance on concentrated
fortress hubs. As for smaller, farther-flung communities, they
predictably pay higher fares—and small cities that rely on concentrated hubs pay even more.

Smaller cities themselves are also at the mercy of the airlines for flight service. Consider Cheyenne, the capital and
most populous city (about 65,000) in Wyoming. Cheyenne had
daily service to Dallas/Fort Worth from American Eagle (part
of American) between 2010 and 2012, when American filed
for bankruptcy. US Airways then bought American, but ended

the Cheyenne route. For a time, Great Lakes Airlines offered a once-weekly turboprop service to Denver, but they ended their service in March 2018. Local leaders who recognized the importance of air service were eventually able to make an agreement for American to resume once-daily flights to Dallas/Fort Worth—so long as the city would guarantee American's revenue to the tune of $2.3 million per year. That same year the airline reported a net profit of $1.4 billion. In April 2020, American ended its route due to the COVID-19 pandemic, once again leaving Cheyenne without commercial air service. In October 2020, local leaders were able to entice United to offer one flight a day to Denver—with the city guaranteeing $850,000 of revenue for the airline.

Notably, Cheyenne is not a participant in the Essential Air Services program (EAS). The EAS was created as part of the Airline Deregulation Act of 1978 to subsidize air travel to small communities after deregulation. Its creation was, in effect, an admission that small cities could suffer from deregulatory dynamics. But the program is woefully insufficient. Very small cities like Cody and Laramie, Wyoming, are covered, but the capital, Cheyenne, is not. The program is also under constant attack from members of Congress who have described it as wasteful spending. Proposals to shrink the $250–$300 million program have included ending eligibility of airports within seventy miles of a larger airport, caps on subsidy amounts, local cost sharing, minimum daily passenger rules, and simply eliminating the program altogether.

The weakness of the program is one of the downsides of the deregulated system for small cities and less populated regions. One of the benefits of the regulated system is that cross-subsidies were built into the fare structure. This was a feature, not a bug, in the system. It meant that smaller cities would get service without constant political battles.

Less-reliable and less-frequent service can be devastating for cities and entire regions. They create a downward spiral that harms the local economy. Think about it this way: if service becomes less frequent, it is not as valuable for passengers—whether tourists or businesspeople—who might need flights more than once a week to a destination. Fewer passengers then mean further reductions in frequency and even higher fares, which in turn mean even fewer passengers. Eventually airlines end the route. For a community, losing routes or losing a hub can be devastating economically. One academic study shows that a 10 percent increase in air traffic creates a 1 percent increase in service-sector employment in an airport's metro area. Others show that hub cities benefit disproportionally from the industry's growth, and that companies choose locations in part based on the frequency and reliability of flights.

In 2011, for example, Chiquita (the banana company) announced that it would move its headquarters from Cincinnati, Ohio, to Charlotte, North Carolina, in part because air service from Cincinnati had become insufficient. Once a hub with many international flights, the number of flights had shrunk and fares increased after airline mergers led to hub consolidation. Pittsburgh, Pennsylvania, was once the home to the annual meeting of K&L Gates, one of the biggest law firms in the country. When flights became too sparse, the firm moved their annual confabs to Washington and New York. The Church of God in Christ had held its annual convention in Memphis, Tennessee, for a hundred years. But with declines in flights in

110   the west Tennessee city, it moved to St. Louis. These examples, as reported by Phillip Longman and now-FTC chair Lina Khan, make clear a critical point: frequent, reliable, affordable air travel is good for business. Each of these cities lost out on huge economic opportunities—headquarters, corporate meetings, conventions—because they didn't have enough flights.

Fortress Hubs

One of the fundamental challenges for competition in the airline industry is the critical importance of airports. Airports, as one scholar has put it, have "economic power that either constitutes or closely resembles monopoly power." Without access to airports, airlines can't fly at all. And constraints on access—how many gates an airline can use, how much each gate costs—can either mean the airline flies frequently to a city or not at all. Airports are a major barrier for a would-be competitive airline. As a result, for dominant carriers, they are also crucial for preserving their power.

Ignoring the critical role airports play was one of the biggest errors of airline deregulation. Advocates thought the airline industry did not have economies of scale and that there were limited barriers to entry into the industry. Airports undermined both of those assumptions. Airports act as hubs, and hub-and-spokes networks create economies of scale. A single flight along a spoke route is more than just a link between two cities; it opens up access to every destination the hub reaches. This means that even if a hub carrier and regional airline operate in the same spoke market, the hub carrier has significant advantages. As one set of scholars puts it, "Hub-spoke network[s] make it difficult for regional carriers to survive."

Courts have also recognized the special economic features of airports. The Department of Transportation, for example, has issued regulations allowing for congestion pricing—higher landing fees for airlines during peak times in order to reduce demand and relieve congestion. When this was challenged in court, a federal appeals court explained that "[i]n an ordinary market, supply and price adjust to eliminate excess demand, but this is no ordinary market. Airports cannot readily increase the supply of landing slots because building more runways takes years and at some airports is not feasible at all."

This, of course, makes airports a barrier to entry: there are only so many runways, gates, and other types of infrastructure available at any one time, and it can take years to build more. Airlines with a long-term lease on gates or with control over slots may also have considerable power to prevent new entrants. To address this problem, the Airport and Airway Improvement Act of 1982 requires that airports that receive funding from the federal government don't discriminate against airlines. Airports must be "available for public use on reasonable conditions and without unjust discrimination," including comparable charges for different airlines. Unfortunately, this provision is written in a way that only the Department of Transportation can enforce it. Airlines that are being treated unfairly are not allowed to bring lawsuits themselves.

In the late 1990s, the FAA and DOT issued a report noting that airlines might engage in anticompetitive delays via "majority-in-interest" clauses. These clauses, which appear in contracts with airlines, allow airlines to reject any new construction project at the airport if they have to pay for some of the financing. These provisions are anticompetitive. They allow airlines with huge market shares at a single airport to prevent new construction projects that could expand the size of the airport and open it up to new competitors. Congress responded to this problem, and passed legislation empowering the transportation secretary to ensure fair and reasonable prices for access to airports.

But even with some federal protections, dominant airlines exercise considerable *informal* power over airport decisions—including by wielding political influence. Consider, as an example, the power of Delta Airlines in Atlanta. Fifty miles away from Atlanta's Hartsfield-Jackson airport is Paulding Northwest Atlanta Airport, a tiny airfield with a two-story building terminal that opened in 2008. The airfield allows ten to thirty departures per day, primarily for recreation or training flights. According to a 2014 report in the *New York Times*, Paulding Northwest applied for a license to fly two commercial flights per week—only to face "stiff opposition" from Atlanta hub dominant carrier Delta Air Lines. Delta "laid out reasons for its opposition in newspaper opinion articles as well as letters to authorities," arguing that Hartsfield-Jackson offered major economic benefits to the region and that there would be downsides for residents and Delta employees if Hartsfield-Jackson grew weaker. Atlanta mayor Kasim Reed came in on the side of Delta, opposing Paulding's desired expansion. Paulding's airport director noted that at most it could handle about ten or twelve commercial flights a week—and that was assuming it opened a second gate. It is hard to see how ten or twelve commercial flights would threaten Delta's employees, the economy of the city of Atlanta, or one of the biggest airlines in the world. But Delta's public pressure campaign may have been a successful attempt to block even the most nascent of potential competitors.

While fortress hubs allow an airline to defend against competitors, they are surprisingly vulnerable when it comes to climate change and cyberattacks. In October 2021, for example, American Airlines canceled 634 flights—more than 12 percent of its total—on a single Sunday. The day before, it canceled 543 flights, more than 10 percent of its total. And the day before that, 342 were canceled and 738 were delayed. The delays and cancellations were due to severe winds at American's hub at Dallas-Fort Worth airport. In an age of climate change and increasingly severe weather events, the hub-and-spokes model makes air travel less resilient. A single weather event at one fortress hub can knock out flights all across the country, creating a cascading set of delays and cancellations that has significant economic and consumer implications.

As critical nodes in a transportation network, a cyberattack at a fortress hub could also have a similarly disastrous cascade effect. One recent study shows that ninety-seven of the top hundred airports in the world failed a basic cybersecurity evaluation. Threats of these types could be mitigated by diffusion across a broader geography. For example, if carriers had merely 25 percent of an airport, rather than 75 percent, they would still benefit from some economies of scale through a hub-and-spokes model, but also not suffer as much disruption in the event that a single airport must shut down.

After Southwest Airlines canceled thousands of flights over the holidays in December 2022, commentators rushed to blame Southwest's route structure, which featured more point-to-point connections than the hub-and-spokes approach of other big airlines. They claimed that Southwest's model was *more* susceptible to disruptions than a hub-and-spokes approach because cancellations cascaded through the system. The real issue was with Southwest's technology, but route design is important for resilience. A hub-and-spokes model increases fragility and decreases resilience because a crisis for a single hub can ground hundreds or thousands of flights. In contrast, whether a point-to-point system is resilient depends on how it is designed. If an airline operates a route from Orlando to New Orleans and then onward to three or four more cities, a cascade of failures is possible if there's bad weather in Orlando. But if the route is a point-to-point route back and forth between Orlando and New Orleans, a problem at Orlando will not cascade any further that New Orleans. Resilience depends on route design.

The Emergence and Failure of Passenger Rights

In 1999, a blizzard in Detroit stranded twenty-four planes and thousands of passengers on the tarmac for eleven hours. Toilets overflowed. The planes ran out of food. The subsequent lawsuits took years. And proposals for "passenger rights" followed: a right to exit, a right to food, water, and restroom use. These proposals failed in Congress, and they failed again in 2007 after further troubles at airports. Why were these proposals needed? Why did they fail?

The short answer is, once again, deregulation. Airline regulation was a form of structural regulation. It organized the operations of the entire industry in a systematic manner, including rates and routes. This meant that competition was based on service quality. Airlines had to offer a better passenger experience

for the same price, because prices were regulated. This led, naturally, to a race to the top on service. Under regulation, a widespread "passenger rights" movement was largely unnecessary
because airlines had no incentive to violate them.

Deregulation flipped these incentives, leading to a reduction in service quality. It is cheaper to offer limited (and worse)
services. With competition on price (at least in some markets),
the incentive to reduce costs grew stronger. Over the following
decades, passenger complaints became commonplace: reduction in meal service, ever-shrinking seats, longer call times with
customer service. With price competition, airlines unbundled
the elements of air travel, and began charging for each component separately—change fees, bag fees, costs for meals. Under
deregulation, airlines also have an incentive to fill planes completely and even to overbook them. This means some passengers could be "bumped" from a flight they had booked. It also
means that rerouting passengers is more difficult in the event
of a delay or cancellation, and even more difficult when there are
multiple simultaneous cancellations at a single hub.

The calls for "passenger rights" began less than a decade
after deregulation, with then congressman (and later secretary
of transportation) Norman Mineta's Air Passenger Protection
Act of 1987, which required creation of a toll-free consumer
hotline, among other things. That bill didn't make it through
Congress. Other proposals, including for a "passenger bill of
rights," failed repeatedly in the 1990s and 2000s.

Passengers also couldn't sue the airlines directly under state
laws. In a series of the cases, the Supreme Court interpreted the
Airline Deregulation Act, which preempted states from enact-
ing or enforcing laws or regulations "relating to rates, routes, or

116   services of any air carrier," broadly to include everything from
deceptive advertising to unfair practices in a frequent flyer program. The court's decisions have been so broad and convoluted
that it even determined that "rates" were at issue when an airline banned a passenger from being in a frequent flyer program.
The purpose of the preemption provision, of course, was to prevent states from undermining deregulation—but the court has
interpreted that provision to disempower passengers.

Change didn't come until the 2010s, when the Department
of Transportation issued a number of regulations protect-
ing consumers. The DOT has the power to address "unfair or
deceptive practices" and ensure "safe and adequate service." The
Obama-era regulations required airlines to disclose the total
cost of a flight (including taxes), allowed passengers to cancel
a flight within twenty-four hours of booking, and gave passengers stronger rights in the case of oversold flights and delays.
But proposals for an airline passenger bill of rights have continued in the face of deteriorating service quality—and they have
continued to fail.

Their failure, too, may be a function of deregulation. After
deregulation and consolidation, the politics of regulating airlines have changed. Passengers are spread across the country
and aren't an easily organized interest group with a trade association or lobbyists in Washington. But they are going up against
a highly concentrated industry with powerful lobbyists. As
scholars have recognized for decades, diffuse majorities have a
more difficult time than concentrated interest groups at achieving their policy preferences in the political process. Indeed, in
the final days of the Trump administration, the Department of
Transportation issued a regulation restricting its own authority

to regulate "unfair or deceptive practices." The airlines lobbied heavily for this rule, in part complaining that the Obama-era regulations were too stringent.

The War for the Skies

Looking back over recent decades, it is easy to see that the attempt to make the airline industry competitive has had many undesirable consequences: geographic inequality, worse service, higher prices, financialization, bailouts, bankruptcies, consolidation. The challenges we all experience when flying stem from a single source: public policy. Without some reasonable boundaries on competition, the airline business is naturally a cutthroat one, in which airlines need to wage war to gain market share and survive. The casualties of this war are virtually every stakeholder who cares about flying: workers, communities, passengers, and the industry itself.

The war for control of the skies is not the fault of the airlines. It is the fault of the public policy choice to place them into a competitive environment with few guardrails. The biggest airlines in the 1970s didn't want to enter into a Hunger Games for survival. Executives like American's Bob Crandall predicted that deregulation would wreak havoc on the industry and on the quality of air travel. Decades later, after American had gone through bankruptcy and been bought by US Airways, its general counsel, Gary Kennedy, remarked: "The business was incredibly exciting, yet chaotic, destined to result in a weak, maimed industry."

How to Fix Flying

Bitter experience is a good teacher. It has been nearly a half-century since airline deregulation, and we have learned a great deal. The airline industry does not work the way that advocates for deregulation thought it would. Unsurprisingly, their predictions—more than a hundred competitive airlines, across-the-board lower prices, no downsides for small communities, little change in service quality, and no chaos in the industry—didn't come true. To their credit, some proponents were willing to admit their errors. But public policy hasn't changed in light of our experience. If we care about small and mid-sized cities, reliable high-quality service, or abuses of monopoly power, we have to address those issues. If we want to make flying less miserable, we will have to change public policy.

But how?

The Political Economy of the Airline Industry

Fixing flying requires a clear-eyed understanding of the economic dynamics of the industry and articulating the social, economic, and political goals for air travel. With more than a century of experience—in three very different policy regimes—we now have a better understanding of these issues than ever before.

The first feature is that air transportation networks are subject to network effects. These network effects manifest in a variety of ways. The value of an airline's network is greater the more locations it serves because travelers can get to more places. Each additional city added to the network is worth more than the route itself; it connects to every other node via the network. The frequency of flights along a route also leads to greater market share. This dynamic reflects how usable the network is. Unlike telephone networks, in which calls can be made at any time, air travel is only possible when planes are scheduled to fly. More frequent service means a more usable, and thus more valuable, network. Passengers want a larger network that has more frequent flights. For a passenger, the ability to travel anywhere at any time, with minimal layovers and without switching air carriers, is beneficial. A larger network reduces transaction costs in terms of purchasing multiple tickets and travel between concourses.

A second feature is economies of scale. Although deregulatory advocates denied the existence of economies of scale, air transportation features critically important economies of scale. First are airport hub-and-spokes networks. Prior to deregulation, major airlines were unable to create fortress hubs at major airports. After deregulation, they did—leading to airport concentration by the end of the 1980s. A large, concentrated hub increases the efficiency of the network because each city connected to the hub connects passengers to every other city the hub services with only one stop at the hub. Importantly, this

120   enables the airline to serve more city pairs with fewer flights. For example, imagine three cities: A, B, and H (for hub). An airline can either connect the three cities with two flights—from A to H and B to H—or with three flights, adding a nonstop flight from A to B. Intermediating flights through the hub allows the airline to forgo additional nonstop flights. Hubs therefore expand network access, while enabling airlines to avoid the added costs of direct flights between points with potentially low passenger volumes.

But at the same time, these hub economies of scale also lead to downsides and fragility for passengers, cities, and the economy as a whole. Concentrated hubs mean fewer direct flights, increasing travel time for passengers—and decreasing their efficiency of movement. They also shrink the number of cities with significant-sized airports. This concentrates economic growth in a small number of fortress hub cities, and denies economic benefits to other cities and regions. Concentrated hubs also make the entire airline network fragile. When one hub goes offline—due to weather or security concerns—it can disrupt the entire airline system in the country. This can have huge economic costs.

A third feature is significant barriers to entry. Airports have physical limitations in the form of the number of runways and gates available, and infrastructural expansions take time. At fortress hubs, dominant air carriers may also exercise informal influence in ways that limit the number of slots available to competitors—possibly even at other airports in the region. These limitations suggest that a new airline would have trouble swiftly entering and competing with the major carriers.

Unrestricted competition isn't sustainable in this industry. In the 1980s, after a brief moment of competition from low-cost carriers, reconsolidation followed. Both mergers and predatory fare wars were standard features of the consolidation playbook in the 1980s and 1990s and since. Big carriers were able to match low prices and outlast new entrants. Doing so even without profit preserved their overall dominance and allowed them to recoup their investments after driving competition out.

Airlines have also adopted policies to enhance the pull of their networks and prevent competition. Frequent flyer programs added additional benefits to staying within the airline network between trips, rather than choosing carriers on a trip-by-trip basis. Over time, partnerships like Oneworld or Star Alliance expanded the size of big carriers' networks globally by granting seamless access to foreign destinations. Computer reservation systems (CRS), created by the big air carriers in the 1980s, facilitated bookings on those airlines, even though travel agents could notionally book individuals on any airline. Self-preferencing within this system operated as a barrier for competitive entry.

The dynamics of regulated and unregulated oligopoly have illuminated challenges with price and non-price competition too. The era of regulated oligopoly was one in which airlines ended up competing aggressively on non-price terms. Some innovations, like new jet technologies, were beneficial. Others, like the availability of piano bars on planes, suggest that the CAB could have reduced prices even in a period of high oil costs and the need for airlines to recoup their investments. The era of unregulated oligopoly has also been one of higher prices and

122   worse service due to low competition along certain routes and common ownership among all the airlines.

What we need are options that take these features of the industry seriously. Instead of wishing away these dynamics, we should harness them to advance public-spirited goals.

The Goals of a New National Airline Policy

From the start, lawmakers have advanced a number of policy aims across the history of air travel: industry development and stability, service reliability, national security, geographic access, passenger experience, and consumer prices. Both advocates for regulation in the 1930s and deregulation in the 1970s acknowledged the importance of these factors—even if they disagreed vehemently on how to achieve them. These factors remain important today.

In its early years, growth of the industry into a stable, reliable, nationwide service was a paramount interest. Air travel was seen as essential for both commercial and national security reasons. To spur development, the federal government subsidized airlines through the airmail program. National security justifications also manifested in other ways, such as restrictions on foreign carriers operating within US territory.

While the *creation* of the airline industry is no longer a concern, its *reliability* remains one. One of the goals of airline regulation was also to ensure that reliable service was available. Air travel is extremely important: it stitches together disparate regions by enabling travel, economic activity, shipping, and communications. One challenge today is that, despite their name, fortress hubs may prove to be remarkably fragile. While fortresses might fend off competitors, they can be vulnerable

to disruptive weather events, cyberattacks, or other geograph-
ically focused shocks. Airport concentration can be a danger to
resilient, reliable service.

A resilient airline industry must also confront and adapt to
climate change and increasingly extreme weather. This means
designing route schedules and structures in a way that mini-
mizes disruption. But it also requires recognizing that air travel
is a major contributor to carbon emissions. A better airline
industry will both contribute less to the problem and do more to
adapt to new realities.

Another challenge has been stability in the industry. Early
advocates wanted to put an end to destructive competition in
the 1930s. Fare wars meant wasted capital expenditures as airlines went bust. Regulatory advocates also sought to avoid a
boom-and-bust cycle, which would disrupt service and labor.
Despite Kahn's later embrace of the destructive side of capitalism, advocates assumed deregulation would not lead to a
boom-and-bust cycle or disrupt the stability of the industry.
Members of Congress also seem to value stability of the industry so highly that they have twice rescued the airlines, despite
airlines making significant profits during the years immediately prior to both September 11 and COVID-19. Instability and
financial insecurity can also push airlines to cut the quality of
service or invent sneaky ways of increasing profits, including
from tacked-on junk fees. Making the industry more stable—
fewer bankruptcies and bailouts, fewer canceled flights—
should be a goal of reform, and it'll also improve the passenger
experience.

Stability also meant labor peace—in the form of good wages
to prevent labor-management disputes. Critics of deregulation

124 worried about labor issues post-deregulation, and their fears were borne out. New competitors offered non-union shops and lower wages, which pushed the big carriers to either create B-scales for new employees or force workers into wage concessions under the threat of bankruptcy or a buyout. These dynamics led to repeated labor strife, including strikes, in the 1980s. Decades later, some major carriers even jettisoned their workers' pensions to the federal Pension Benefit Guaranty Corporation (PBGCs). The COVID-19 early retirement packages and subsequent worker shortages show how important skilled pilots, flight attendants, ground crews, and other airline employees are. Reforms should keep in mind that workers in the airline industry deserve a fair deal for their employment— and that they are skilled workers who cannot be easily replaced. Having a stable airline workforce is critical to safe and reliable service.

Both regulatory and deregulatory advocates have also valued access to air transportation. A central aim has been to ensure air transportation nationwide, in order to connect people and commerce. The initial policy goal of subsidies (and then regulation) to develop an airline industry, including passenger travel, was partly to achieve the goal of expanding access. Without widespread availability, Americans would not benefit from what was then a new technology. In the 1970s, the debate over access shifted from mere availability to the cost of air travel, as deregulators criticized the high prices that the CAB had adopted via rate regulation. Indeed, the CAB does seem to have undervalued the possibility that lower prices would mean a greater volume of air travel. Ensuring that we have fair prices that ensure access to air travel is critical.

Access has also manifested in the form of geographic considerations. Under structural regulation, geographic access was achieved via route allocation, the "equal fares for equal miles" approach to pricing, and the system of cross-subsidies within the airlines. These policies facilitated air service to many smaller markets. Proponents of deregulation also supported the goal of geographic access, claiming that their reforms would not harm rural and small community access. To ensure those communities did not lose service, they created the Essential Air Service subsidy program. But this approach has not been successful. Cities like Cheyenne, Wyoming, neither get air service from the market nor receive EAS subsidies, and thus are left to find the money on their own to guarantee the revenue of highly profitable airlines. The other consequence of these dynamics, coupled with airport consolidation into fortress hubs, is to widen geographic inequality between regions. Well-connected airports spur economic growth, and when a community loses air service, it can negatively affect the local economy. Fostering access to air travel and the economic growth that comes with it is therefore another important aim of national airline policy.

With these dynamics and goals in mind, we can identify three principles for fixing flying.

1. **No More Flyover Country.** Air travel is critical to commerce and opportunity. We need air service to be available all across the country, including in mid-sized and smaller cities.
2. **No Bailouts, No Bankruptcies.** We need a stable, reliable, resilient, and innovative airline industry that

doesn't suffer from boom-and-bust cycles. We need it to work all the time, not just when the economy is good.

3. **Fair and Transparent Pricing.** We need a pricing system that achieves both of the above goals—and that doesn't push airlines to create complicated fare structures with hidden conditions or tacked-on fees.

Importantly, if we keep these principles in mind, we'll also achieve a range of other goals. A stable industry is good for workers. Coupling that with fair and transparent pricing is good for improving the passenger experience. If we get the *structure* of a new national airline policy right, we can fix flying—without a lot of complicated regulations for the industry and without a miserable experience for passengers.

So how do we turn these principles into public policy?

A National Airline

One possibility is to embrace the fact that the airline industry tends toward consolidation. Taken to its logical conclusion, this approach suggests that air travel should be a monopoly—with a single carrier flying everywhere.

Every few years, a popular writer will suggest nationalizing the airlines. The most recent calls followed the COVID-19 airline rescue in 2020. In the United States, some advocates for nationalization focus on the economic dynamics of the industry: the four big airlines face little competition (with 80 percent market share), had been extremely profitable in the years leading up to the COVID-19 pandemic, and spent their profits on stock buybacks, before asking for government support when demand dropped. If airlines needed public support during downturns, the argument goes, then the public should take control and get the upside as well. Nationalization would end the "too big to fail" bailouts. Other advocates for nationalization focus on how the industry intersects with important social goals. In particular, one UK commentator argued that nationalization could help combat climate change by enabling emissions reductions. A comprehensive, unified transportation strategy would optimize choices across air, rail, and transit, in order to minimize carbon emissions.

From the perspective of the long history of airline regulation and deregulation, one of the benefits of nationalization is that it would create a single, unified system. A single national carrier, with no private competitors, would benefit from network effects and economies of scale to a greater degree than even a four-firm oligopoly. Passengers, in turn, would never have to ask which airline serves a location—every airport would be in the national carrier's network. A national carrier would also be able to price at system cost because it would not need to make a profit. It could also cross-subsidize rural and smaller communities.

The downside of nationalization is that such a system might suffer from declining service quality due to the lack of competition. It is unclear whether this would be likely. For example, until legislative constraints were placed on it, the US Postal Service (another national monopoly characterized by network effects and featuring cross-subsidies) was highly innovative. But it is possible that a nationalized airline would become sclerotic.

128   A Regulated Monopoly

An alternative to a single federally operated national airline is to contract with a single private firm for the operations of the airline. In other words, to take air transportation seriously as a single public utility. This approach would be distinct from the approach taken under CAB regulation. During that period, the CAB allowed *multiple* airlines to compete as a regulated oligopoly. Under a single public utility approach, there would only be one airline, a regulated monopoly—just as there are usually regulated monopolies for water, sewer, and electric providers. The regulated monopoly airline would be privately capitalized, saving the government the effort of funding the airline. But the structure of the deal would look more like a contracting agreement than regulated competition. The government would specify the terms of service and regulate rates.

A single public utility airline would benefit, like a national carrier, from economies of scale and scope and network effects throughout the system. Unlike during the era of regulated oligopoly, the regulated monopoly airline would not need to compete with other airlines on service quality, which is what led to absurd offerings like piano bars. The primary downsides are first that the government would need an administrative apparatus to monitor the airline—to oversee the contract and evaluate operations—as compared to simply running it, in the case of nationalization. Second, as with a nationalized system, the airline might also suffer from fewer quality of service improvements due to a lack of competition. Here, too, it is not clear if that would happen. When AT&T was the single, regulated monopolist for telephone service in the mid-twentieth century, it offered high quality service and was extraordinarily

innovative through its Bell Labs division. One could easily
imagine a public utility airline replicating that model and creating an "Air Labs" division to focus on cutting-edge technological developments for air travel.

A Public Option
A third possibility is to combine competition and public
provision—and create a public option for air travel. On this
model, a national carrier would operate alongside one or more
private carriers, each of which would adhere to some identical
terms of service. For example, each airline would have to serve
all locations in the network and have to follow some basic safety
and service standards. But the airlines would compete on other
terms: price and other qualities of service. The existence of a
public option might also bring benefits to passengers, in that
they would have a reliable carrier that would offer a simple service without as much customization and complexity as private
carriers.

A two-airline public option model would maximize the
benefits of network effects and economies of scale for both airlines while still offering competition. It might also be superior
to a purely private duopoly, because the public option airline
would not have an interest in colluding with the private airline
to raise prices and lower service quality. Indeed, some studies of
public-private duopoly show that competition between public
and private can spur competition in both directions.

Something like this approach was tried in Australia until
that country deregulated its airline industry in 1990. Under the
"two airline policy," a public and private airline competed with
each other. Both were subject to stringent regulations: serving

130   identical routes, on (roughly) identical schedules, with identical planes, at identical rates. Even under those stringent conditions, the system of head-to-head public-private competition was effective, and both public and private airlines were financially viable. This suggests that it is unlikely that the public option would simply undercut the private option. Of course, there may be features of Australia's geography that are inapplicable to the United States. Notably, while deregulation in Australia brought in new competitors, the most prominent failed within fifteen months. Commentators concluded that the Australian market is a natural duopoly.

A public option operating in an oligopolistic environment, as the United States is currently, would be unlikely to succeed, unless all airlines were required to serve all locations. Private options would most likely shift even more toward serving high-profit, low-cost, and high-volume routes, leaving the public option to serve the highest-cost, lowest-volume routes. Without rate and route regulation, cream-skimming would mean that the public option would perennially be unable to compete with the private oligopoly—and it would likely mean high profits to legacy firms and high costs for the public.

Regulated Competition

Moving to a system of public airlines—whether a single national carrier, a single private carrier regulated as a public utility, or a public option—would be a significant change from how airlines currently work. It might be an efficient and effective way to achieve the principles of a new national airline policy, while accepting at face value what we know about the economic dynamics of the industry. But it also has downsides. For those who want to preserve a system of multiple private airlines, there are ways to improve upon our current system. Of course, moving toward regulated competition will also have some downsides: it would not solve all of the structural problems in the sector; it could end up as a whack-a-mole solution in which powerful airlines maneuver around the regulations; and it could become a "kludgy" solution that is hard to administer and bogs the airlines (and regulators) down in complicated rules that are hard to implement effectively. But if designed well, many of these downsides can be minimized or avoided altogether.

No More Flyover Country

To help ensure access throughout the country, airlines must have a duty to serve smaller cities that would not otherwise get air service. Because smaller cities have fewer travelers, prices based on the cost of those flights are higher. Higher prices, in turn, reduce the demand for service. The regulated system of the twentieth century addressed the problem by authorizing the CAB to allocate routes and set rates. But this model didn't work very well. Route allocation proceedings were complicated and took years to conclude, as did rate-setting. There are, however, simpler and more competitive ways to solve the problem of access.

One way to address the problem of cities like Dubuque, Iowa, and Cheyenne, Wyoming, losing service would be to establish a new system of regional and national carriers. Under this "Regional Conference System," Congress would divide up the country into some number of regions (e.g., New England, the Southeast, the Midwest) and separate local flights from major-city flights. The big national carriers would continue

132   to fly and compete between big cities all across the country, including between the biggest cities within each region. But within each region, a single new airline would make direct flights between small cities, medium cities, or between a large city and smaller cities.

Here's how it would work. In each region, a new airline—say, "Southern Airlines"—would get an exclusive federal license to operate all flights within the region. The price of flights would be regulated under the traditional approach, the cost of service plus a rate of return. Every major carrier would have the ability to interconnect with the regional airline, so passengers on American or Delta or United could fly to the smaller cities without buying multiple tickets on different airlines or needing to recheck their baggage. This approach would have some significant benefits. First, it would guarantee service to a much greater number of cities—places like Dubuque and Cheyenne. Second, it would expand the number of direct flights within regions, reducing the need for people to spend hours driving for short trips or routing through hubs. At present, for example, there are no direct flights between Nashville, Tennessee, and Jackson, Mississippi (six hours, fifteen minutes driving), or Asheville, North Carolina (four hours, thirty-eight minutes driving). A new "Southern Airlines" could provide such flights. Third, this approach is neither full regulation nor full deregulation— regional service would be regulated to ensure its future. Major city service would be unregulated, allowing for competition among the current big-four oligopoly. Fourth, many of these regional flights would operate on smaller planes, and innovation leading to clean energy airplanes is more likely to come first to smaller planes than larger ones.

Another option would be for Congress to reform the Essential
Air Service program to ensure that all cities of a reasonable size
have access to air service. Instead of subsidizing a set of towns
for air service—which leaves some cities, like Cheyenne, with
neither service nor a subsidy—Congress could require every
major airline to serve a set of smaller communities. Call this
the "Draft-Pick System." Congress would establish criteria for
cities that are covered under the program, including popula-
tion above a certain size, state capitals, distance from the near-
est city, and other factors. The Department of Transportation
would then compose a list of eligible cities. Every five years,
the biggest airlines (which could be defined by the number of
routes) would participate in an NFL-style draft. By lottery, airlines would receive a pick order, and then be able to pick any city
from the list. They would be required to offer regular service to
that city from multiple places at a regulated rate. The government would offer no subsidies, and thus have no reason to arti-
ficially limit the number of cities in the program. Airlines would
cross-subsidize their Draft-Pick routes from profits elsewhere
in their system. Because there would not be rate regulation out-
side of the Draft-Pick cities, airlines would still be free to compete over prices and charge whatever they like elsewhere in the
system. They would also be free to choose Draft-Pick cities
based on network efficiencies, such as distance to nearby hubs.
In order to prevent cream-skimming, airlines would also have
an exclusive license to serve the Draft-Pick cities.

No Bailouts, No Bankruptcies
A stable, thriving, and reliable airline industry is also critical. It's
good for the companies, their workers, and for the country. But

134 after the post-9/11 bailouts and the COVID payroll support program, airlines know that they can capture the private benefits of profits during good times, and avoid the downsides when there is an economic crisis. One simple way to solve this problem would be for lawmakers to refuse to bail out the airlines the next time there is a crisis that leads to plummeting demand. That approach would force airlines to find additional options in the capital markets for financing, declare bankruptcy, or make different choices in their profitable years on how to spend their profits. But this strategy has big downsides. Airlines are an essential service that is critical to national security and commerce. We ideally don't want them to go through bankruptcy proceedings, even if they won't be liquidated. Given the importance of airlines to the economy and to our society, it is thus unlikely that lawmakers will stand firm and refuse to bail out the airlines.

One answer is that Congress could require each airline to create a "rainy day" fund and a crisis mitigation plan. A mandatory rainy-day fund would address the problem of saving during flush years. Every airline would be required to save for a crisis, which means none of them would be at a competitive disadvantage for saving. This fund could then be tapped when payroll support is needed or to otherwise help rescue airlines that are in trouble, when there is a serious demand-shock. Airlines could also be required to create crisis mitigation plans, in which they model what they would do if there is another demand shock—like a war, economic crash, or pandemic—how they would ensure reliable service during the crisis, and how they would rebuild capacity afterward. Of course, it is possible that if the crisis is bad enough, the airlines' plans wouldn't work and they might still ask for a bailout. But the likelihood will be far lower

if airlines were required to have funding on hand and to have
planned for crises.

In addition, we should deconcentrate fortress hubs. Introducing more competition into major airports would mean some reduction in efficiency for specific airlines, but would also likely result in greater system resiliency, lower prices, and reductions in geographic inequality. Resilience would be improved because the shutdown of a single airport would have less of an effect on each airline's overall operations because they would have greater ability to reroute through other airports. Given that studies have shown that prices to and from fortress hubs are higher than along more competitive routes, greater competition in major airports would likely bring prices down. If airlines were limited to, for example, 25 percent market share at any major airport, it might push them to increase the number of hubs across the country. Rather than having a few major hubs, they might develop a larger number of hubs to gain the benefits of scale that a hub-and-spokes network provides. This would bring further economic growth and development to other cities, which would also help reduce geographic inequality.

Note that a more stable airline industry—in the form of some protected routes, as described above, fewer fortress hubs, and a rainy day fund—would help workers and passengers by making air travel more reliable. But Congress should also ensure that airlines do not use competitive dynamics or economic crises as a way to pressure their workers to take pay cuts. Having a skilled, stable workforce in the airline industry is essential to reliable service. Pilots, flight attendants, and even call-center operators cannot be trained overnight. A system that leads to furloughs and layoffs, or cuts to pay and benefits, is unlikely to

136   be one that retains talented workers. With so few airlines having such a large market share, Congress could require a system of
sectoral standards among the airlines and their workers. Instead
of bargaining airline by airline over wages, benefits, and hours
(and with some airlines excluded), there could simply be a single standard for the whole sector. Airlines therefore could not
compete with each other by cutting pay and benefits for workers. They'd have to find savings elsewhere or focus on innovation to make service better. This is particularly important given
how few airlines there are, and how interlinked they are. Pilots,
flight attendants, machinists, and others simply do not have
many options.

A thriving airline sector is one that also innovates. In con-
junction with a "rainy day" fund, Congress could also require that
airlines put aside some money into a mandatory Air Innovation
Fund. The funding would be used to create Bell Labs—style
innovative hubs to work on ways to make flying more innovative. For example, scalable technologies to wean airplanes off jet
fuel are essential. While there are companies that are attempting to electrify planes or use biofuels, more research and development is essential to make progress on this goal.

Fair and Transparent Prices

One of the benefits of these reforms is that they will help passengers all around the country. Rate regulation based on an
"equal fares for equal miles" principle would ensure that
prices are fair, uniform, and transparent to Draft-Pick cities
or when flying a regional airline under the conference system.
Deconcentrating hubs will increase competition and should
therefore reduce prices.

The federal government should ensure that airline pricing is fair, simpler, and more transparent. Federal officials could bring cases under the antitrust laws to end common ownership, which economists have shown raises prices. Professor Einer Elhauge argues that horizontal shareholding is actionable today under the Clayton Act. Others suggest that the Department of Transportation can address common ownership under section 411(a) of the Federal Aviation Act, which empowers DOT to address "an unfair method of competition in air transportation."

Congress could also go further and require that seats are priced uniformly regardless of when seats are purchased and within (a limited number of) service classes. This would prevent the proliferation of gradations like "comfort plus" and prevent airlines from pricing dynamically based on how soon the flight is. This is similar to pricing in other transportation utilities: prices to take subways or buses don't change if you buy your ticket a week in advance or right before you get on. Congress could also place limits on additional fees for services that airlines provide. There should be a basic level of service—including baggage and seating—that applies to everyone, with a transparent price so people can easily compare fares. Finally, Congress or the Department of Transportation could push for airlines to increase transparency around their loyalty programs, including disclosing how those programs work, what the exchange rates are between points and dollars, and requiring notice before making changes to those rates.

These reforms won't solve everything, but they are attentive to the economic dynamics of the industry and draw inspiration from the American tradition of regulated capitalism.

138 Together, they would go a long way in restructuring the airline industry so that it operates more like a public utility.

How We Get There

Whatever you think is the best way to fix flying, the key lesson is this: there is nothing natural, magical, or inevitable about the way we run our airlines. Delays don't have to be so common. Geographic access doesn't have to be so limited. Service quality doesn't have to be so low. All it will take to fix the system is for people to change it—just like we subsidized airlines in the early years, just like we built the regulated system in the 1930s, and just like we deregulated it in the 1970s.

Congress could pass any of the changes described here immediately. These reforms should command bipartisan support. After all, mid-sized cities like St. Louis and Toledo and states with large rural populations like Wyoming and West Virginia are hurt by the current failures of airline policy. Both businesspeople and ordinary travelers are harmed by complicated fare structures, limited routes, and delays and cancellations. Both workers and shareholders do well when the airlines are stable and thriving.

So the next time your flight is delayed or canceled, your bags are lost, or you're frustrated at paying a high price for a small seat, remember that it doesn't have to be this way. You can ask your members of Congress to take action. You can ask your candidates running for office to commit today to acting when they get into power. And you can keep pushing and pressuring them until they actually do it.

Flying doesn't have to be miserable. We can fix it.

Reviving the American Tradition of Regulated Capitalism

The history of airline regulation and deregulation shows that we lost a great deal in abandoning the American tradition of regulated capitalism. For generations—centuries even—policymakers understood that some sectors of the economy were special. These sectors required a different kind of governance system in order to make sure that monopolies and oligopolies wouldn't harm the public or provide poor and unreliable service.

The deregulation of networks, platforms, and utilities was part of a broader set of economic trends over the last half-century. Scholars have called this period "the neoliberal era," with economic policy defined by deregulation, trade liberalization, privatization, and fiscal austerity. In specific arenas, neoliberal economic ideas have come under sustained fire in recent years. The financial crisis galvanized opposition to deregulatory efforts in that sector. Scholars and elected officials increasingly argue that the paradigm of antitrust law that emerged with Robert Bork in the 1970s should be abandoned. Political leaders on the left and right have called for an aggressive industrial policy and have been more willing to consider trade restrictions, rather than further globalization. And scholars and political movements have become more prominent in advancing public provision of social goods, rather than privatization.

In the context of this broad rethinking of the approach that dominated over the last half-century, a fresh look at airline deregulation calls into question the neoliberal assault on the American tradition of regulated capitalism. In the mid-twentieth century, a number of scholars, many associated with the Chicago School, attacked structural regulation. Their efforts were profoundly important, setting the stage for economywide deregulation. Some of the Chicago School's foundational research has since been debunked—including some by their own fellow travelers. But the American tradition of regulated capitalism has not yet recovered from that assault.

The history of airline regulation and deregulation offers additional reasons to revive the American tradition of regulated capitalism. Many of the claims and theories that advocates of deregulation advanced were proven wrong in the following decade—and deregulators like Kahn admitted as much. Indeed, it is hard not to read Kahn's account today as deeply influenced by an ideological preference for unregulated capitalism—no matter the consequences. When outcomes were contrary to other stated goals (e.g., rural service, worker wages, service quality), Kahn's position was simply that those effects were an inevitable consequence of competition. In some cases, he went so far as to say that even caring about those goals was illegitimate.

But considering only the aims and claims of the deregulators, airline deregulation was a failure. Average prices went down after deregulation at about the same rate they were declining before deregulation. Even Kahn admitted that prices did not decline across the board—and in some cases actually increased. Meanwhile, forty years later, the deregulatory advocates' claims about competition in the sector are at best laughable. They suggested that some 200 airlines could operate competitively; that there was no possibility of full airplanes and high profits; and that the sector had limited barriers to entry and economies of scale. That a huge and essential part of the economy was radically transformed in a matter of just a few years based on such an inaccurate understanding of the industry is shocking—and it should condemn the underlying theories.

But airlines weren't the only area that saw radical deregulation over the last generation. Deregulatory advocates also took aim at railroads, buses, trucking, ocean shipping, telecommunications, banking, and energy. In each of these areas, they abandoned the American tradition that helped make the United States the most successful economy of the twentieth century. The result, of course, has not been effective competition. It has been a new age of monopoly capitalism.

Railroads had been the industry that pushed Congress to create the Interstate Commerce Act and inaugurated federal regulation of transportation. In the mid-twentieth century, American cities were connected by rail lines that sent passengers all across the country. Competition from trucking and airlines hurt the railroads, but so did deregulation in 1980. As in airlines, deregulation led to consolidation and a drive to cut costs. Between 1980 and 2022, the number of railroads dropped from forty to seven—and four of the seven have between an 83 and 90 percent market share. To cut costs, the big railroads

142 focused on profitable lines, shifted freight to companies without unions, shrunk the labor force (from 500,000 to 135,000), and moved to a system of precision scheduled railroading (PSR), which involves longer trains and less spare capacity. Prices are up, along with profits. By the time of the pandemic, the deregulated, consolidated railroad system failed to deliver resilient service—supply chain shortages were partly due to the fragility of the industry.

Telecommunications have not fared much better. Deregulation combined with antitrust to break up the regulated monopolist AT&T. But after a period of competition, there was consolidation once again. In the broadband arena, the lack of structural regulation has meant a small number of providers with extraordinary power. It is little surprise that Comcast, now Xfinity, is regularly one of the most disliked companies in America. For people in rural America, broadband access—like electricity and other utilities—is a necessity. But under the deregulated system, the market hasn't provided high quality access. Recent legislation is instead pouring billions of dollars into subsidizing the creation of rural broadband networks. From the perspective of the national interest, why should we have a system of disliked, highly profitable monopolies and taxpayer subsidies, instead of a regulated system where costs are lower and access is universal?

Changes in the energy sector have caused their share of problems as well. The marketization of the production-transmission-distribution process has created extraordinary complexity. Energy marketplaces have been characterized by speculation and arbitrage, causing the blackouts and energy crisis in California in the early 2000s. The Texas power outages

as a result of a winter storm in 2021 led to hundreds of deaths,
millions in economic losses, and days of disruption. Climate
change requires that the energy system change significantly,
and it is not at all clear that the current approach will do enough
to address that challenge.

Finally, in the banking sector, deregulation had the most
obvious, devastating consequences. Less than a decade after
Congress ended structural separations, allowed banks to grow
to behemoth size, and deregulated derivatives, speculation and
runs on the money markets caused the 2008 global financial
crisis. Instead of living in a country with thousands of small,
boring banks, we have a small number of "too big to fail" banks
that got bailed out after the crash. And after another round of
deregulation in 2018, in 2023, a major bank once again failed—
requiring the federal government to promise to backstop unin-
sured depositors.

And yet, despite the extraordinary failures of public policy
in all of these areas, the American tradition of regulated capitalism remains largely dead even as a matter of academic research
and study. Few textbooks have been written in the field over the
last forty years, and perhaps the most prominent academic article in the field of "regulated industries" during the last quarter century was, in effect, a eulogy. Meanwhile, policymakers
are hesitant to use regulation as a tool for achieving valid and
important public purposes. In many cases, they seem to have
simply forgotten that structural regulations exist as an option.

At the same time, antitrust law has seen a spirited, if controversial, revival. The neo-Brandeisian movement, named
after Progressive Era antitrust advocate and Supreme Court justice Louis Brandeis, is moving beyond the paradigm that defined

144 antitrust in the neoliberal era. But the history of airline deregulation also shows the limitations of reviving antitrust alone.
Kahn, of course, blamed the neoliberal revolution in antitrust
for airline consolidation. But the political economy of the sector
suggests that unfettered competition is the wrong framework
for governing airlines. Air travel is more similar to other infrastructural or public utility sectors than it is to selling chairs or
coffee mugs. Airlines benefit from network effects and economies of scale. They face barriers to entry. And destructive competition and predatory fare wars were common—at least until
the sector consolidated into a small number of mega-carriers,
who now share significant amounts of common ownership.

Antitrust and regulation are two sides of the same coin. In
some areas, competition can work. In others, it won't work. And
when it doesn't, the primary ways to prevent abuses of power
are to nationalize the industry or regulate it. The American tradition has focused on regulating capitalism. Regulations made
sure that important infrastructural goods were available to
everyone across our vast country—on fair terms, with reliable
and high-quality service, and in a way that ensured workers,
companies, and communities succeeded. Politicians these days
may invoke *regulation* as a bad word. But the American tradition
has recognized that regulation is often the only way to avoid
capitalism's abusive tendencies while harnessing its benefits.

This book emerged from a larger project to revive and refashion the law governing networks, platforms, and utilities (NPUs)—what I describe in the book as the American tradition of regulated capitalism. I cannot thank my coauthors in that work, Morgan Ricks, Shelley Welton, and Lev Menand, enough for their intellectual partnership on such an ambitious venture and for their comments and suggestions.

Many others provided helpful feedback on and support for this book. Chris Serkin has been a helpful interlocutor and coauthor, especially on issues of geographic inequality. Lisa Bressman, Richard John, Bob Kuttner, and Sean Seyer were generous enough to read the entire manuscript and offer comments. Participants in a workshop on the NPU casebook, including Paul Dempsey and Andrew Goetz, offered helpful suggestions on the airlines chapter. I am also very grateful to Joe DePete, Taylor Garland, Henry Harteveldt, Lina Khan, Gary Leff, William McGee, Barbara Peterson, Brett Snyder, and Matt Stoller for helpful conversations over the years. Meredith Capps and Clanitra Nejdl in the Vanderbilt Law Library were heroic in tracking down sources and helping with research. Nick Lemann, Jimmy So, and Camille McDuffie offered terrific feedback and shepherded this book through the publication process with ease.

My dad spent many years during his career flying all over the world; my father-in-law, Pat, is an air traffic controller; and my wife, Alison, traveled among three cities on two continents in the early years of our relationship. This book is dedicated to the three of them and to my mom and my mother-in-law, Pam, who have spent more time hearing about flights and airport issues than they probably ever imagined.

The most fun starting points on the history of airline policy are a couple of riveting journalistic accounts of deregulation and its aftermath—Thomas J. Petzinger, *Hard Landing: The Epic Contest for Power and Profits That Plunged the Airlines into Chaos* (1995), and Barbara Sturken Peterson and James Glab, *Rapid Descent: Deregulation and the Shakeout in the Airlines* (1994). I drew heavily from Peterson and Glab's terrific book and highly recommend it.

On the early history of airlines, I recommend F. Robert van der Linden, *Airlines and Air Mail: The Post Office and the Birth of the Commercial Aviation Industry* (2002); Sean Seyer, *Sovereign Skies: The Origins of Civil Aviation Policy* (2021); and Alan P. Dobson, *FDR and Civil Aviation: Flying Strong, Flying Free* (2011). The FAA published an official history of airline policy, which provides an excellent overview of that agency's predecessors and its operations from the early years into the 1970s. The books in this series are available on the FAA's website and include Nick A. Komons, *Bonfires to Beacons: Federal Civil Aviation Policy Under the Air Commerce Act, 1926–1938* (1978); John R. M. Wilson, *Turbulence Aloft: The Civil Aeronautics Administration Amid Wars and Rumors of Wars, 1938–1953* (1979); Stuart I. Rochester, *Takeoff at Mid-Century: Federal Aviation Policy in the Eisenhower Years, 1953– 1961* (1976); Richard J. Kent, *Safe, Separated, and Soaring: A History of Federal Civil Aviation Policy, 1961–1972* (1980); and Edmond Preston, *Troubled Passage: The Federal Aviation Administration During the Nixon-Ford Term, 1973–1977* (1987).

On deregulation, the Kennedy subcommittee's report is an astonishing document, well worth reading critically. Civil Aeronautics Board Practices and Procedures, Report of the Subcommittee on Administrative Practice and Procedure of the Committee on the Judiciary, S. Rep. 60-316, 94th Cong., 1st Sess. (1975). Thomas K. McCraw's *Prophets of Regulation* (1984) offers a biography of Alfred Khan. One of the best short overviews of airline regulation and deregulation is Richard H. K. Vietor, "Contrived Competition: Airline Regulation and Deregulation, 1925–1988," *Bus. Hist. Rev.* 64 (1990), 61. On the consequences of deregulation, Paul Dempsey's and Andrew Goetz's works are essential, including *Airline Deregulation and Laissez-Faire Mythology* (1992); Paul Stephen Dempsey, "The Rise and Fall of the Civil Aeronautics Board—Opening the Floodgates of Entry," *Transp. L.J.* 11 (1979), 91; Andrew R. Goetz and Christopher J. Sutton, "The Geography of Deregulation in the U.S. Airline Industry," *Ann. Ass'n Am. Geo.* 87 (1997), 238; and Andrew R. Goetz and Timothy M. Vowles, "The Good, The Bad, and The Ugly: 30 Years of Airline Deregulation," *J. Transport Geo.* 17 (2009), 251.

William J. McGee's *Attention All Passengers* (2012) offers an excellent history and analysis of the issues facing passengers—from prices to safety.

For those interested in the American tradition of regulated capitalism, or networks, platforms, and utilities law, I must recommend my own book with Morgan Ricks, Shelley Welton, and Lev Menand, *Networks, Platforms, and Utilities: Law and Policy* (2022), from which portions of this book are drawn, but with significant revisions. For a pre-deregulation text, William K. Jones's casebook *Cases and Materials on Regulated Industries* (1976) is excellent. Bruce Wyman's two volume *The Special Law Governing Public Service Corporations* (1911) remains an essential treatise on the topic from more than a century ago.

INTRODUCTION

11   **more than 180,000 flights were canceled:** "Airline On-Time Statistics and Delay Cause," Bureau of Transportation Statistics, January–November 2022, https:// www.transtats.bts.gov/OT_Delay /ot_delaycause1.asp?qv52ynB =qn6n&20=E; Kyle Arnold, "Flight Cancellation Tally Nears 2,500 for the Week at DFW Airport, Dallas Love Field," *Dallas Morning News*, January 31, 2023.

15   **number of major airlines has shrunk:** William J. McGee, *Attention All Passengers: The Airlines' Dangerous Descent—and How to Reclaim Our Skies* (2012), 6.

15   **predicted they would never lose money ever again:** "Leslie Josephs, American Airlines CEO: 'I Don't Think We're Ever Going to Lose Money Again,'" CNBC, September 28, 2017.

15   **more than its annual payroll in a given year:** Matthew Stuart and Clancy Morgan, "Airline Salaries Compared to Stock Buybacks Show Why So Many People Are Angry at the Bailout," *Insider*, April 3, 2000. For a discussion of the particulars on American's choice, see Adam Levine-Weinberg, "'Airlines' Didn't Waste All Their Cash Flow on Share Buybacks: American Airlines Did," *Motley Fool*, March 25, 2020.

15   **passenger travel was down 96 percent:** "Lessons from CARES Act Aviation Loans," GAO, December 2020, https://www.gao.gov/assets /gao-21-198.pdf.

15   **would not liquidate the company or significantly disrupt air travel:** Veronica de Rugy and Gary D. Leff, "The Economic Case Against a Second Airline Payroll Bailout," Mercatus Center, George Mason University, October 2, 2020, https://www.mercatus.org /publications/corporate-welfare /economic-case-against-second -airline-payroll-bailout.

16   **American took $12.74 billion:** Author calculations based on Treasury data, available at: Payroll support payments: https://home .treasury.gov/policy-issues /coronavirus/assisting-american -industry/payroll-support -program-payments; Payroll support extension payments PSP2 (Consold. Approps. 2021): https:// home.treasury.gov/policy-issues /coronavirus/assisting-american -industry/payroll-support -program-extension-payments; Payroll support extension program PSP3 (ARP 2021): https://home .treasury.gov/policy-issues /coronavirus/assistance-for -american-industry/payroll -support-program/psp3.

16   **airlines offered early retirement and voluntary furloughs:** Kyle Arnold, "39,000

American Airlines Workers Take Early Retirement, Leave or Reduced Hours in Face of Covid-19 Pandemic," *Dallas Morning News*, April 30, 2020, https://www.dallasnews.com/business/airlines/2020/04/30/39000-american-airlines-workers-take-early-retirement-leave-or-reduced-hours-in-face-of-covid-19-pandemic/; Tracy Rucinski and David Shepardson, "U.S. Major Airlines Roll Out More Options to Avoid Staff Layoffs," Reuters, May 28, 2020, https://www.reuters.com/article/us-health-coronavirus-airlines-usa/u-s-major-airlines-roll-out-more-options-to-avoid-staff-layoffs-idUSKBN2342U6.

16   almost twice as many cancellations in 2022, as compared to the average over the prior decade: Author calculations, excluding 2020, based on https://www.transtats.bts.gov/homedrillchart.asp.

16–17   fatigue rates were 350 percent higher than before the pandemic: Andrew Curran, "Southwest Airlines' Pilot Union Warns of Flight Crew Fatigue," *Simply Flying*, April 13, 2022; Joe Kunzler, "Labor Relations at Southwest Airlines Are Becoming More Turbulent," *Simply Flying*, October 5, 2022.

17   some airlines had more pilots than before COVID: "Pilot Supply by the Numbers," ALPA Fact Sheet,

2022, https://www.alpa.org/-/media/ALPA/Files/pdfs/advocacy/alpa-pilot-supply-by-numbers.pdf?la=en.

17   the biggest US carriers only started pilot training programs in the last few years: Peter Greenberg, "Why Is There a Pilot Shortage? It Wasn't Just the COVID-19 Pandemic," CBS News, July 21, 2022, https://www.cbsnews.com/news/why-is-there-a-pilot-shortage-covid-retirements-training/; Jennifer Alsever, "Why Is There a Pilot Shortage? 6 Factors That Are Contributing to the Airline Industry Crisis," *Fast Company*, July 26, 2022, https://www.fastcompany.com/90772392/why-is-there-a-pilot-shortage-6-factors-that-are-contributing-to-the-airline-industry-crisis.

17   American cut 28,000 flights—17 percent of its flights in November: Ollie Gratzinger, "How American Airlines Cuts to Its Flight Schedule Will Impact Pittsburgh Travelers," *Pittsburgh* magazine, August 15, 2022, https://www.pittsburghmagazine.com/how-american-airlines-cuts-to-its-flight-schedule-will-impact-pittsburgh-travelers/.

17   American, Delta, and United have dropped fifty-nine cities from service: Taylor Rains and Bianca Giacobane, "American, Delta, and United Have Collectively Dropped 74 US Airports Since the

150   Pandemic—See the Full List,"
      Business Insider, updated April 5,
      2023, https://www.businessinsider
      .com/see-full-list-of-airports-us
      -airlines-dropped-since-2020
      -2022-9.

**17   In the 1970s, Toledo had
service from five carriers:** David
Jacobs, "'Sad to See This Go': Last
Flight Out Marks End of Era at
Toledo Express," *Toledo Blade*,
September 6, 2022, https://www
.toledoblade.com/local
/transportation/2022/09/06/last
-flight-out-marks-end-era-toledo
-express/stories/20220906130.

CHAPTER ONE

**23   developed an unmanned
aircraft that he called an
"aerodrome":** David Kindy, "This
Odd Early Flying Machine Made
History but Didn't Have the Right
Stuff," *Smithsonian Magazine*, May
5, 2021.

**23   would always be as rapid
as the fastest mode of
communication possible:** The old
adage was that "[t]he celerity of the
mail should always be equal to the
most rapid transition of the
traveler." See, e.g., *Report of the
Postmaster General* (1882), 226
(quoting report of Postmaster
General W. T. Barry, November 1,
1834).

**23   which the Army operated for a
few months before the Post Office**

took over: William M. Leary, *Aerial
Pioneers: The U.S. Air Mail Service,
1918–1927* (1985).

**23   with foreign countries
investing in the development of
airlines:** Sean Seyer, *Sovereign
Skies: The Origins of American Civil
Aviation Policy* (2021), 37.

**23   passed the Airmail Act of
1925 (also known as the Kelly
Act):** 43 Stat. 805.

**23   the act was poorly designed
and problems emerged almost
immediately:** Frederick A. Ballard,
"Federal Regulation of Aviation,"
Harv. L. Rev. 60 (1947), 1235,
1241–43.

24   Air Commerce Act of 1926: 44
Stat. 568.

**24   trying to fix the problems in
the Kelly Act:** 45 Stat. 594.

**24   the industry got caught up in
a "speculative boom":** *Report of
the Antitrust Subcommittee of the
House Committee on the Judiciary
on Airlines,* 85th Cong., 1st Sess.
(1957), quoted in William K. Jones,
*Cases and Materials on Regulated
Industries* (2nd ed., 1976), 1073–74.

**24   Airlines were proliferating
quickly, and some were operating
at a loss:** F. Robert van der Linden,
*Airlines and Air Mail: The Post
Office and the Birth of the
Commercial Aviation Industry*
(2002), 97, 106–9, 112.

24–25   **One set of smaller airlines that combined during this period became American Airways:** F. Robert van der Linden, *Airlines and Air Mail.*

25   **and simultaneously save money for the Post Office:** M. Houston Johnson V, *Taking Flight: The Foundations of American Commercial Aviation 1918–1938* (2019), 93; F. Robert van der Linden, *Airlines and Air Mail*, 153.

25   **the McNary-Watres Act:** 46 Stat. 259.

25   **to determine how to consolidate routes and merge firms together:** F. Robert van der Linden, *Airlines and Air Mail*, 153.

25   **Brown found a work-around:** M. Houston Johnson V, *Taking Flight*, 97; Nick A. Komons, *Bonfires to Beacons: Federal Civil Aviation Policy Under the Air Commerce Act, 1926–1938* (1978), 205–10.

25   **led quickly to the creation of major airlines TWA and United:** Alan P. Dobson, *FDR and Civil Aviation* (2011), 13.

26   **corrupt "spoils conferences":** U.S. Senate, Special Committee to Investigate Air Mail and Ocean Mail Contracts. Thomas Petzinger Jr., *Hard Landing: The Epic Contest for Power and Profits That Plunged the Airlines into Chaos* (1995), 9.

26   **Brown's work took on the atmosphere of scandal:** John T. Correll, "The Air Mail Fiasco," *Air Force Mag.* (March 2008), 51, 64–65.

26   **had conspired to prevent competitive bidding:** Frederick A. Ballard, "Federal Regulation of Aviation," 1246–47.

26   **shifted all airmail operations to the Army Air Corps:** John T. Correll, "The Air Mail Fiasco," 64–65.

26   **backtracked immediately amid public outcry:** John T. Correll, "The Air Mail Fiasco," 64–65.

26   **Airmail Act of 1934:** 48 Stat. 933.

27   **"engaged directly or indirectly in any phase of the aviation industry":** Sec. 7(a).

27   **separated into United Air Lines and the Boeing Aircraft Company:** F. Robert van der Linden, *Airlines and Air Mail*, 289.

27   **were awarded similar routes to those they had previously flown:** F. Robert van der Linden, *Airlines and Air Mail*, 284.

27   **to take advantage of demand from increasing passenger travel:** Frederick A. Ballard, "Federal Regulation of Aviation," 1251.

28   **rivalry between nations had led to government support:** M. Houston Johnson V, *Taking*

152   *Flight*, 154–56; Nick A. Komons,
       Bonfires to Beacons, 15.

28   **is the traditional American
way:** Paul Stephen Dempsey, "The
Rise and Fall of the Civil
Aeronautics Board—Opening the
Floodgates of Entry," *Transp. L.J.* 11
(1979), 91, 96, note 11.

37   **In January 1935, the Federal
Aviation Commission issued its
report:** Federal Aviation
Commission, S. Doc. No. 15, 74th
Cong., 1st Sess. (1935), 61–62.

37   **that would encourage the
development of a stable, well-
functioning airline industry:** Civil
Aeronautics Bill, House Rep. 2254,
75th Cong., 3rd Sess. (1938), 1–2.

38   **we are dealing with an infant
industry:** Paul Stephen Dempsey,
"The Rise and Fall of the Civil
Aeronautics Board—Opening the
Floodgates of Entry." Note that one
of the justifications for airline
regulation was stability in the
industry in order to serve the
national defense. In a 1939 speech,
Franklin Roosevelt explained the
value of the statute:

> Underlying the statute is the
> principle that the country's
> welfare in time of peace and its
> safety in time of war rest upon
> the existence of a stabilized
> aircraft production, an
> economically and technically
> sound air transportation system
> both domestic and overseas—an

> adequate supply of well-trained
> civilian pilots and ground
> personnel.
> This new national policy set up
> by the Congress views American
> aviation as a special problem
> requiring special treatment.

Alan P. Dobson, *FDR and Civil
Aviation*, 76. By the 1970s, of
course, the national security
context differed considerably,
including the need to mobilize
airlines and pilots.

38   **prevent the spread of bad
practices and of destructive and
wasteful tactics:** Civil Aeronautics
Act of 1938, Sen. Rep. No. 1661, 75th
Cong., 3rd Sess. (1938), 2.

39   **system has completely
broken down in recent months:**
Civil Aeronautics Bill, House Rep.
2254, 75th Cong., 3rd Sess. (1938),
1–2.

40   **aimed to enable airlines
to "operate on a stable basis":**
Civil Aeronautics Bill, House Rep.
2254, 75th Cong., 3rd Sess. (1938),
1–2.

40   **financially secure airlines
would also have little reason to
compromise on safety standards:**
William K. Jones, *Cases and
Materials on Regulated Industries*,
1081.

40   **Civil Aeronautics Act of
1938:** 52 Stat. 973. For helpful

accounts of the legislative history of the act, see Joseph C. Mahoney, "Legislative History and the Right of Entry in Air Transportation Under the Civil Aeronautics Act of 1938," *J. Air L. & Com.* 20 (1953), 330, 332–33; Howard C. Westwood and Alexander E. Bennett, "A Footnote to the Legislative History of the Civil Aeronautics Act of 1938 and Afterword," *Notre Dame Lawyer* 42 (1967), 309.

41 "required by the public convenience and necessity": § 401(d).

41 to navigate between open entry in air transportation: Report of the Antitrust Subcommittee of the House Committee on the Judiciary on Airlines, 85th Cong., 1st Sess. (1957), in William K. Jones, *Cases and Materials on Regulated Industries*, 1083.

41 weighed multiple criteria when determining public convenience and necessity for new routes: See, e.g., Trans-Southern Inc. et al.—Certificate of Public Convenience and Necessity, 2 C.A.B. (1940), 250, 253–54.

41 the CAB again weighed multiple factors: Paul Stephen Dempsey, "The Rise and Fall of the Civil Aeronautics Board—Opening the Floodgates of Entry," 109, 111–12; see also William K. Jones, *Cases and Materials on Regulated Industries*, 1102–4 (discussing

practical questions of route allocation).

42 but it also simultaneously denied new entrants flight routes: Richard H. K. Vietor, "Contrived Competition: Airline Regulation and Deregulation, 1925–1988," *Bus. Hist. Rev.* 64 (1990), 61, 69–72.

42 increase enforcement to prevent cream-skimming by the non-scheduled airlines: John R. M. Wilson, *Turbulence Aloft: The Civil Aeronautics Administration Amid Wars and Rumors of Wars 1938–1953* (1979), 161–62.

42 airline industry comprised "trunk" carriers and local service carriers: Emmette S. Redford, *The Regulatory Process* (1969), 145.

42 by 1953, ten of the thirteen trunk carriers no longer needed government support: Stuart I. Rochester, *Takeoff at Mid-Century: Federal Civil Aviation Policy in the Eisenhower Years, 1953–1961* (1976), 29.

42 cut the number of city-pairs (that is, routes): Richard H. K. Vietor, "Contrived Competition," 61, 69–72.

42 it failed to authorize a single new entrant from 1950 to 1974: Paul Stephen Dempsey, "The Rise and Fall of the Civil Aeronautics Board—Opening the Floodgates of Entry," 109, 115.

154   43   **expanding the routes of existing carriers, rather than authorizing new carriers:** Samuel B. Richmond, *Regulation and Competition in Air Transportation* (1961), 71–72.

43   **the other "trunk" line carriers doubled their collective market share:** William K. Jones, *Cases and Materials on Regulated Industries*, 1091.

43   **"any unjust discrimination or any undue or unreasonable prejudice or disadvantage in any respect whatsoever":** Civil Aeronautics Act of 1938, section 404 (b). For a discussion, see Richard E. Caves, Air Transport and Its Regulators 160 (1962).

43   **because the airlines agreed to lower prices:** Emmette S. Redford, *The Regulatory Process*, 150.

44   **it authorized discounted fares to spur more demand:** Mark H. Rose, Bruce E. Seely, and Paul F. Barrett, *The Best Transportation System in the World: Railroads, Trucks, Airlines, and American Public Policy in the Twentieth Century* (2006), 84–87.

44   **"designing and buying even bigger, faster, and more exciting airplanes":** Thomas Petzinger, Jr., *Hard Landing*, 16.

44   **so airlines were taking on higher debt levels and earning lower returns:** Richard H. K. Vietor,

"Contrived Competition," 71–75, 77.

45   **agreed to cut their fuel usage by 5 percent:** Edmund Preston, *Troubled Passage: The Federal Aviation Administration During the Nixon-Ford Term, 1973–1977* at 70–75 (1987).

45   **meant the CAB would again have to increase prices:** Richard H. K. Vietor, "Contrived Competition," 71–75, 77.

46   **got taken to court for conducting a closed-door proceeding:** See *Moss v. CAB*, 430 F.2d 891 (D.C. Cir. 1970).

46   **would first consider the costs and revenues on an industrywide basis:** Paul Stephen Dempsey, "The Rise and Fall of the Civil Aeronautics Board—Opening the Floodgates of Entry," 115–17.

46   **sought to address the crisis in the airline industry by reducing excess capacity:** Richard H. K. Vietor, "Contrived Competition," 77–79.

46   **Continental served complimentary Chivas Regal in coach:** Thomas Petzinger Jr., *Hard Landing*, 20.

CHAPTER TWO

48   **attacked the reasoning behind the American tradition of regulated capitalism:** For an

overview with application to airline deregulation, see Binyamin Appelbaum, *The Economists' Hour: False Prophets, Free Markets, and the Fracture of Society* (2019), 161–84.

49   academic studies arguing that fares would be lower without regulation: See, e.g., William A. Jordan, *Airline Regulation in America* (1970); Michael E. Levine, "Is Regulation Necessary? California Air Transportation and National Regulatory Policy," *Yale L.J.* 74 (1965), 1416.

49   government agencies were "captured" by the industries they regulated: See generally Paul Sabin, *Public Citizens: The Attack on Big Government and the Remaking of American Liberalism* (2021) (describing Nader's efforts and those of his followers and supporters).

49   argued that airline deregulation would reduce "big government": Martha Derthick and Paul J. Quirk, *The Politics of Deregulation* (1985), 47.

50   "a cartel, a simple cartel being organized by the government": Barbara Sturken Peterson and James Glab, *Rapid Descent: Deregulation and the Shakeout in the Airlines* (1994), 33–35.

50   "Let's get rid of the CAB": Thomas Petzinger Jr., *Hard Landing*, 80–81.

51   who concluded that Gingery   155
committed suicide and closed the case: Barbara Sturken Peterson and James Glab, *Rapid Descent*, 41–43.

51   emerging anti-regulation ideology that both Democrats and Republicans would ultimately embrace: For more on the importance of Democrats joining Republicans on deregulation, see Ganesh Sitaraman, *The Great Democracy: How to Fix Our Politics, Unrig the Economy, and Unite America* (2019).

51   "led to 'adequate, economical and efficient service by air carriers at reasonable charges'": The rest of this section summarizes the CAB report: Civil Aeronautics Board Practices and Procedures: Report of the Subcommittee on Administrative Practice and Procedure of the Committee on the Judiciary, S. Rep. 60-316, 94th Cong., 1st Sess. (1975), 1 [hereinafter Report].

56–57   where he brought this approach to reforming electricity and telephone prices: For an overview of Kahn's life and beliefs, see Thomas K. McCraw, *Prophets of Regulation* (1984), 222–99.

57   constrained by the statute from taking more radical measures: Paul Stephen Dempsey and Andrew R. Goetz, *Airline Deregulation and Laissez-Faire Mythology* (1992), 179–87.

156

57 **to prevent both destructive competition and possible monopolization:** See Civil Aeronautics Act of 1938, § 401(d); see also supra Part A.1.

57 **adopted an experimental policy called "multiple permissive entry":** Paul Stephen Dempsey and Andrew R. Goetz, *Airline Deregulation and Laissez-Faire Mythology*, 179–87.

57 **"executing the sentence first, then getting around to holding the trial":** Barbara Sturken Peterson and James Glab, *Rapid Descent*, 48.

57–58 **the CAB acted swiftly across multiple areas at once:** Paul Stephen Dempsey, "The Rise and Fall of the Civil Aeronautics Board—Opening the Floodgates of Entry," 94.

58 **to "scramble the eggs" so they could not be put back together after the fact:** Paul Stephen Dempsey, "The Rise and Fall of the Civil Aeronautics Board—Opening the Floodgates of Entry," 94; Kahn said: "We are going to get the airline eggs so scrambled that no one is ever going to be able to unscramble them." Barbara Sturken Peterson and James Glab, *Rapid Descent*, 48.

58 **launching no-frills, no-meals (only peanuts) service:** Barbara Sturken Peterson and James Glab, *Rapid Descent*, 59–63, 68.

59 **Airline Deregulation Act of 1978:** 92 Stat. 1705.

59 **"no community will lose air service as a result of this bill":** Senate Committee Report 95-631, S. 2493, February 6, 1978, in Comm. Public Works & Transp., U.S. House of Reps., Legislative History of the Airline Deregulation Act of 1978 (May 1979), 396–97.

59 **In the short term, it is reasonable to expect more flights:** Senate Committee Report 95-631, S. 2493, 392.

59 **"You fucking academic pinhead!":** The exact quote is contested. Barbara Sturken Peterson and James Glab, *Rapid Descent*, 49, report this is what Crandall said. Thomas Petzinger Jr., *Hard Landing*, 91, reports that Crandall called them "eggheads," not "pinheads."

60 **The CAB would then be dissolved:** Paul Stephen Dempsey and Andrew R. Goetz, *Airline Deregulation and Laissez-Faire Mythology*, 195–96.

60 **awaiting their chance to get access to dormant routes:** Paul Stephen Dempsey and Andrew R. Goetz, *Airline Deregulation and Laissez-Faire Mythology*, 195–96.

61 **declared its broad support for an open entry system:** "Las Vegas-Dallas/Fort Worth Nonstop

Service Investigation," CAB Order 78-7-116 (1978), 5.

61   **"a reduction or loss of service to the southeast Alaska communities and bush points":** "Southeast Alaska Service Investigation," CAB Order 79-4-168 (1979), 7–8.

62   **the CAB still awarded multiple entry:** "Iowa/Illinois-Atlanta Route Proceeding," CAB Order 78-12-35 (1978).

62   **to "avoid practical problems that new entrants could pose to airport authorities":** "Austin/San Antonio-Atlanta Service Investigation," CAB Order 79-3-9 (1979), 9–10. Note that airport congestion is a barrier to entry— something that advocates for deregulation argued did not exist in the industry.

62   **if a low-cost carrier entered markets with financially secure airlines:** "Oakland Service Case," Order 78-4-121, at 25–26, 37, 42–44, 68, 77 (1978); "Las Vegas-Dallas/Fort Worth Nonstop Service Investigation," CAB Order 78-7-116 (1978), 4. Paul Stephen Dempsey, "The Rise and Fall of the Civil Aeronautics Board—Opening the Floodgates of Entry," 130–32.

62   **"the Board . . . is unnecessarily and . . . woodenly":** CAB Order 79-3-9 (1979) (dissent, at 1).

62   **the *Milwaukee Show-Cause*   157 *Proceeding*:** A show-cause proceeding allowed CAB to issue an order without holding an evidentiary hearing, on the theory that there were no complex issues or material facts that needed to be addressed. See Paul Stephen Dempsey and Andrew R. Goetz, *Airline Deregulation and Laissez-Faire Mythology*, 204.

63   **not in the best interest of the consumers, the carriers, and the communities of our country:** CAB Order 79-3-13 (1979) (dissent at 4-6).

64   **requiring merely that an applicant show they had a *plan* for getting financing:** Paul Stephen Dempsey and Andrew R. Goetz, *Airline Deregulation and Laissez-Faire Mythology*, 206–8; Paul Stephen Dempsey, "The Rise and Fall of the Civil Aeronautics Board—Opening the Floodgates of Entry," 166.

64   **"an aspiring entrepreneur need only show that in a set of perfect circumstances the proposed operations could be feasible":** "Transcontinental Low-Fare Route Proceeding," CAB Order 79-1-75 (1979) (dissent at 1–2).

65   **United Airlines reported that 58 of their 327 city-pair routes were unprofitable:** Report, 66.

158   65   **existing carriers may have a significant advantage:** Report, 69.

66   **would be a highly competitive world with flexible prices:** Report, 67–68.

67   **described California from 1946 to 1965:** William A. Jordan, *Airline Regulation in America* (1970).

67   **"airlines that could efficiently provide travelers with the service and price they wanted were successful":** Report, 48.

67   **entry restriction is designed to prevent:** Morgan Ricks, Ganesh Sitaraman, Shelley Welton, and Lev Menand, *Networks, Platforms, and Utilities: Law and Policy* (2022), ch. 1.

68   **believed their airline would succeed *precisely because* it could undercut the federally regulated prices:** Thomas Petzinger Jr., *Hard Landing*, 24–26.

68   **the law explicitly said that federal regulation only applied to airlines traveling between states:** *Texas Int'l Airlines v. Civil Aeronautics Board*, 473 F.2d 1150 (D.C. Cir. 1972).

CHAPTER THREE

69   **"The Closest Thing to War in Peacetime":** The source for this section is Barbara Sturken Peterson and James Glab, *Rapid Descent*, 84–216.

77   **two titans in the airline sector looked back over these battles and engaged in a heated debate:** Alfred E. Kahn, "Surprises of Airline Deregulation," *Am. Econ. Rev.* 78 (1988), 316; Melvin A. Brenner, "Airline Deregulation: A Case Study in Public Policy Failure," *Transport. L.J.* 16 (1988), 179; Alfred E. Kahn, "Airline Deregulation: A Mixed Bag, but a Clear Success Nevertheless," *Transport. L.J.* 16 (1988), 229; Melvin A. Brenner, "Rejoinder to Comments by Alfred E. Kahn," *Transport. L.J.* 16 (1988), 253. The literature on deregulation during and after this period is extensive. The focus here on the Kahn-Brenner debate is largely due to the importance of Kahn's role in deregulation and his admission of its many problems. Other important evaluations include Steven Morrison and Clifford Winston, *The Economic Effects of Airline Deregulation* (1986); and Steven A. Morrison and Clifford Winston, *The Evolution of the Airline Industry* (1995).

77   **even advocates for deregulation were deeply surprised:** Alfred E. Kahn, "Surprises of Airline Deregulation," 316.

78   **higher than before deregulation:** Andrew R. Goetz and Christopher J. Sutton, "The Geography of Deregulation in the U.S. Airline Industry," *Ann. Ass'n Am. Geo.* 87 (1997), 238, 239.

78   **the increased likelihood, in consequence, of monopolistic exploitation:** Alfred E. Kahn, "Surprises of Airline Deregulation," 318 (citations omitted).

78   **"developing and dominating hubs":** Alfred E. Kahn, "Surprises of Airline Deregulation," 318.

79   **benefits airlines that fly to more places:** For an argument that the costs of such programs were built into fare prices and suggesting that such programs are undesirable, see Michael W. Tretheway, "Frequent Flyer Programs: Marketing Bonanza or Anti-Competitive Tool?" *J. Transp. Res. F.* 30 (1989), 195. See also Melvin A. Brenner, "Airline Deregulation: A Case Study in Public Policy Failure," 184, 186.

79   **they could discount their fares to levels that smaller competitors couldn't match:** Alfred E. Kahn, "Surprises of Airline Deregulation," 318.

79   **footnote:** Thomas Petzinger Jr., *Hard Landing*, 126–27. Carrier-Owned Computer Reservation Systems (Final Rule), 49 Fed. Reg. 32540 (August 15, 1984). Computer Reservation System (CRS) Regulations (Final Rule), 69 Fed. Reg. 976 (January 7, 2004). For a discussion, see Cindy R. Alexander and Yoon-Ho Alex Lee, "The Economics of Regulatory Reform: Termination of Airline Computer Reservation System Rules," *Yale J. on Reg.* 21 (2004), 369.

79   **"theory of contestable markets":** Melvin A. Brenner, "Airline Deregulation: A Case Study in Public Policy Failure," 188, 194. The classic on the theory of contestable markets was not published until after airline deregulation. See William J. Baumol, John C. Panzer, and Robert D. Willig, *Contestable Markets and the Theory of Industry Structure* (1982), but it was important to the case for deregulation. See, e.g., Lawrence J. White, "Economies of Scale and the Question of Natural Monopoly in the Airline Industry," *J. Air L. & Com.* 44 (1978), 545, 548.

80   **"were misled by the apparent lack of evidence of economies of scale":** Alfred E. Kahn, "Surprises of Airline Deregulation," 318. Of course, the hub arguments were raised prior to deregulation. The subcommittee dismissed them, suggesting they were unlikely to happen, and if they did, they might in fact be desirable. Report, 71–72.

81   **airlines that have greater frequency increase their market share disproportionately:** Urs Binggeli and Lucio Pompeo, "Analyst Viewpoint: Does the S-Curve Still Exist?" IATA, September 2006.

81   **it is referred to as having a "fortress hub":** For contemporary

160   data on fortress hubs, see James Pearson, "The Battle of the Big US Hubs: American vs Delta vs United," *Simple Flying*, August 18, 2021.

81   **the fault lay with the Department of Transportation:** Alfred E. Kahn, "Airline Deregulation: A Mixed Bag, but a Clear Success Nevertheless," 234. See also Steven A. Morrison and Clifford Watson, Airline Deregulation and Public Policy, *Science* 707 (1989), 245.

81   **made it inevitable that the industry would eventually consolidate:** Melvin A. Brenner, "Rejoinder to Comments by Alfred E. Kahn," 259.

82   **published *The Antitrust Paradox*:** Robert Bork, *The Antitrust Paradox* (1978).

82   **even if that meant allowing more mergers and consolidation:** For discussions of the Chicago School, see, e.g., Richard A. Posner, "The Chicago School of Antitrust Analysis," *U. Pa. L. Rev.* 127 (1978), 925; Herbert J. Hovenkamp and Fiona Scott Morton, "Framing the Chicago School of Antitrust Analysis," *U. Pa. L. Rev.* 168 (2020), 1843.

82   **pushed the Reagan administration to "prune" antitrust law:** Matt Stoller, "The Secret Plot to Unleash Corporate Power," *Big*, Substack, April 8, 2022.

83   **for decades, people would point to the expansion and growth of the industry:** For a later account that describes surface-level data on industry expansion, see Government Accountability Office, GAO-06-630, *Airline Deregulation: Reregulating the Airline Industry Would Likely Reverse Consumer Benefits and Not Save Airline Pensions*, June 2006, 10–12.

83   **nearly doubled again by 1978:** Airlines for America, "U.S. Airline Traffic and Capacity," March 10, 2023, https://www.airlines.org /dataset/annual-results-u-s -airlines-2/.

83   **airlines had gone from above water by 1 percent to underwater by 2 percent:** Melvin A. Brenner, "Airline Deregulation: A Case Study in Public Policy Failure," 199, 201, 206.

84   **the losses in the later 1980s were a function of competition:** Alfred E. Kahn, "Surprises of Airline Deregulation," 316–17.

84   **significantly lower wages for new employees:** Thomas Petzinger Jr., *Hard Landing*, 145.

85   **"You said the unions were going to support deregulation":** Barbara Sturken Peterson and James Glab, *Rapid Descent*, 245.

85 **"part of the price we are usually willing to pay for the benefits of a competitive economy":** Alfred E. Kahn, "Airline Deregulation: A Mixed Bag, but a Clear Success Nevertheless," 243.

85 **more passengers traveled on discount tickets:** Alfred E. Kahn, "Surprises of Airline Deregulation," 319. Of course, the question was not whether a ticket was characterized as "discount" but what the actual fare levels were.

86 **the price benefits stemming from deregulation had diminished:** Melvin A. Brenner, "Airline Deregulation: A Case Study in Public Policy Failure," 195–96, 198.

86 **footnote:** Alfred E. Kahn, "Airline Deregulation: A Mixed Bag, but a Clear Success Nevertheless," 235. Melvin A. Brenner, "Rejoinder to Comments by Alfred E. Kahn," 253.

87 **there was no reason to think that had regulation remained:** Melvin A. Brenner, "Rejoinder to Comments by Alfred E. Kahn," 254–55 and fig. 1.

88 **"Reregulating the Airline Industry Would Likely Reverse Consumer Benefits and Not Save Airline Pensions":** GAO, *Airline Deregulation: Reregulating the Airline Industry Would Likely Reverse Consumer Benefits and Not Save Airline Pensions.*

88 **both advocates and critics of deregulation agreed on one thing:** Alfred E. Kahn, "Surprises of Airline Deregulation," 319.

88 **footnote:** GAO, *Airline Deregulation: Reregulating the Airline Industry Would Likely Reverse Consumer Benefits and Not Save Airline Pensions.*

89 **fares in the denser markets have gone down, dramatically:** Alfred E. Kahn, "Airline Deregulation: A Mixed Bag, but a Clear Success Nevertheless," 237.

89 **source of these disparities was how much competition:** Melvin A. Brenner, "Airline Deregulation: A Case Study in Public Policy Failure," 195, 198.

89 **Markets with more competition faced lower prices than those with less competition:** Other studies confirmed these findings, showing that concentrated hubs had higher fares than unconcentrated airports, and that where mergers led to a decline in competition, fares rose. For a discussion, see Paul Stephen Dempsey and Andrew R. Goetz, *Airline Deregulation and Laissez-Faire Mythology* (1992), 333–34.

89 **"some parts of the public get bargains":** Melvin A. Brenner, "Airline Deregulation: A Case Study in Public Policy Failure," 195, 198.

162

90 **largely conceded the point about geographic price differences:** Alfred E. Kahn, "Airline Deregulation: A Mixed Bag, but a Clear Success Nevertheless," 236.

90 **he opposed the idea that there was a reverse cross-subsidy at work:** Alfred E. Kahn, "Surprises of Airline Deregulation," 320.

90 **footnote:** Paul Stephen Dempsey, "Corporate Pirates Assault the Heavens—Leveraged Buy-Outs and the Airline Industry," *DePaul Bus. L.J.* 2 (1989), 59, 61.

90 **earning zero revenue from an empty seat:** Melvin A. Brenner, "Airline Deregulation: A Case Study in Public Policy Failure," 192–93, 204.

91 **resources going to aircraft maintenance dropped 30 percent:** Paul Stephen Dempsey and Andrew Goetz, "Airline Deregulation Ten Years After: Something Foul in the Air," *Journal of Air Law and Commerce* 54, no. 4 (1989), 957.

92 **could have a "systemwide chain reaction" on the whole airline nationally:** Melvin A. Brenner, "Airline Deregulation: A Case Study in Public Policy Failure," 213.

92 **"these discomforts are a sign of the success of deregulation, not its failure":** Alfred E. Kahn, "Surprises of Airline Deregulation," 320.

92 **travelers preferred lower fares coupled with worse service:** Modern commentators share this sentiment. See, e.g., Matthew Yglesias, "Why Flying in America Keeps Getting More Miserable, Explained," *Vox*, April 12, 2017.

92 **"not a single community that enjoyed a minimum level of certificated service":** Alfred E. Kahn, "Surprises of Airline Deregulation," 317.

93 **"see the air service into their [s]tates declining precipitously":** The Economic Impact of Federal Airline Transportation Policies on East Tennessee: Hearing Before the S. Comm. on the Budget, 99th Cong. 44 (1985) (statement of Sen. Jim Sasser).

93 **[T]his is one Senator who regrets that he voted for airline deregulation:** 132 Cong. Rec. 5107 (March 18, 1986) (statement of Sen. Robert Byrd).

93 **smaller cities had fewer nonstop flights:** Melvin A. Brenner, "Airline Deregulation: A Case Study in Public Policy Failure," 189, 209, 211.

93 **some smaller communities were better off even without nonstop service:** Melvin A. Brenner, "Airline Deregulation: A Case Study in Public Policy Failure," 189, 209, 211. Other scholars came to similar conclusions. See, e.g., Thomas Gale Moore, "U.S. Airline

Deregulation: Its Effects on Passengers, Capital, and Labor," *J.L. & Econ.* 29 (1986), 1, 15, 18 (noting that 40 percent of small cities lost service and that small cities saw increases in prices).

94 adequacy, convenience, and reasonable pricing of its airline service: Melvin A. Brenner, "Airline Deregulation: A Case Study in Public Policy Failure," 189, 209, 211.

94 willing to pay the price of instability in order to encourage creativity, innovation, and continuous improvement: Alfred E. Kahn, "Airline Deregulation: A Mixed Bag, but a Clear Success Nevertheless," 246–47.

95 "'[P]artial re-regulation' is, I suggest, just about as feasible as partial pregnancy": Alfred E. Kahn, "Airline Deregulation: A Mixed Bag, but a Clear Success Nevertheless," 239.

95 it was better suited to a "partial 'public utility' approach": Melvin A. Brenner, "Airline Deregulation: A Case Study in Public Policy Failure," 183, 186.

95 rejected out of hand the goals and benefits of the American tradition of regulated capitalism: Melvin A. Brenner, "Airline Deregulation: A Case Study in Public Policy Failure," 181–83. (The "inherent disposition to resent

government interference and to favor free markets" had led to "a general tendency to overstate the favorable accomplishments of deregulation and to downplay its defects.")

CHAPTER FOUR

96 safety did not precipitously decline: See Andrew R. Goetz and Timothy M. Vowles, "The Good, the Bad, and the Ugly: 30 Years of Airline Deregulation," *J. Transport Geo.* 17 (2009), 251, 254–60.

96 it became subject to boom-and-bust cycles: See Andrew R. Goetz and Timothy M. Vowles, "The Good, the Bad, and the Ugly: 30 Years of Airline Deregulation," 251, 254–60.

97 With the price up, Trump cashed out and walked away: Barbara Sturken Peterson and James Glab, *Rapid Descent*, 228, 233.

98 The United deal fell apart, and Trump dropped his bid for American: Barbara Sturken Peterson and James Glab, *Rapid Descent*, 257–66.

98 raised fuel costs and created fears of terrorism: Evelyn Thomchick, "The 1991 Persian Gulf War: Short-Term Impacts on Ocean and Air Transportation," *Transp. J.* 33 (Winter 1993), 40, 44.

98 had left some airlines with high debt-to-capital ratios: Paul

164   Stephen Dempsey, "Corporate Pirates Assault the Heavens—Leveraged Buy-Outs and the Airline Industry," *DePaul Bus. L.J.* 2 (1989), 59, 64, 65; General Accounting Office (GAO), Airline Competition: Weak Financial Structure Threatens Competition, GAO-RCED-91-110 (April 1991).

98   **more than all the profits they had made since the 1920s combined:** Barbara Sturken Peterson and James Glab, *Rapid Descent*, 277–79, 293, 298.

99   **will tend to keep passengers as long as there is price parity:** Michael E. Levine, "Airline Competition in Deregulated Markets: Theory, Firm Strategy, and Public Policy," *Yale J. Reg.* 4 (1987), 393, 476.

100   **"If you are not going to get them out[,] then no point to diminish profit":** *United States v. AMR Corp.*, 140 F. Supp. 2d 1141 (D. Kan. 2001).

100   **pushback from airlines who claimed this was the first step down a slippery slope:** Eric M. Patashnik, *Reforms at Risk: What Happens After Major Policy Changes Are Enacted* (2008), 127.

100   **"But here, it engaged only in bare, but not brass, knuckle competition":** *United States v. AMR Corp.*, 140 F. Supp. 2d 1141 (D. Kan. 2001).

101   **had their pension plans bailed out by the federal Pension Benefit Guaranty Corporation:** Andrew R. Goetz and Timothy M. Vowles, "The Good, the Bad, and the Ugly: 30 Years of Airline Deregulation," 251, 254–60.

101   **Air Transportation Safety and System Stabilization Act:** 115 Stat. 230.

101   **approved the US Airways application swiftly and ultimately rejected those of United:** Margaret M. Blair, "The Economics of Post-September 11 Financial Aid to Airlines," *Ind. L. Rev.* 36 (2003), 367, 369, 385, 390, 392.

101   **By the late 2000s, another wave of consolidation was underway:** Andrew R. Goetz and Timothy M. Vowles, "The Good, the Bad, and the Ugly: 30 Years of Airline Deregulation," 254–60; Thomas Pallini, "Airline Mergers and Acquisitions in the US Since 2000," *Business Insider*, March 21, 2020.

102   **"unfettered competition just doesn't work very well in certain industries":** Terry Maxon, "All Hail, Bob Crandall," *Dallas Morning News*, April 17, 2009.

102   **Star Alliance had 100 percent market share between Frankfurt, Germany, and Newark:** John F. O'Connell, "The Global Airline Industry," in *The Routledge*

Companion to Air Transport Management (eds. Nigel Halpern and Anne Graham, 2018), 17.

102   **the law had long prohibited cross-ownership within "any phase of aeronautics":** See, e.g., CAA, § 408.

102   **banned horizontal shareholding, interlocking directorates, and conglomeration more broadly:** Sections 7 and 15 of the Airmail Act of 1934.

102   **were critical components of the Civil Aeronautics Act of 1938:** Sections 408, 409, and 412 of the Civil Aeronautics Act of 1938.

102   **ultimately repealed by the Civil Aeronautics Board Sunset Act of 1984:** Sections 26, 27, 30, and 40 of the Airline Deregulation Act and sections 3, 4, and 9 of the Civil Aeronautics Board Sunset Act of 1984.

103   **they also owned 27.5 percent of Delta, 27.3 percent of JetBlue, and 23.3 percent of Southwest:** Einer Elhauge, "Horizontal Shareholding," *Harv. L. Rev.* 129 (2016), 1267, 1267–69.

103   **further concentrated through these "common owners":** For more on common ownership, see C. Scott Hemphill and Marcel Kahan, "The Strategies of Anticompetitive Common

Ownership," *Yale L.J.* 129 (2020), 1392; Madison Condon, "Externalities and the Common Owner," *Wash. L. Rev.* 95 (2020), 1.

103   **"96 percent of their cash profits on stock buybacks to enrich investors and their own executives":** Henry Grabar, "Why Do Airlines Need a Bailout?" *Slate*, March 17, 2020.

103   **CARES Act:** Pub. L. No. 116-136, Sec. 4114.

105   **private shareholders get all the upside in the profitable years:** For a discussion of the elements of "too big to fail" arguments, see Ganesh Sitaraman, "Unbundling Too Big to Fail," *Center for American Progress,* July 15, 2014; see also Saule Omarova, "The 'Too Big to Fail' Problem," *Minn. L. Rev.* 103 (2019), 2495.

105   **Airlines create frequent flyer points out of thin air, and then sell them to banks:** Joann Muller, "Why Airlines Are Going Overboard to Win Your Loyalty," *Axios*, March 6, 2022.

106   **have recently removed some of their award charts, making rates opaque:** J. T. Genter, "How Airlines Make Billions from Monetizing Frequent Flyer Programs," *Forbes,* July 15, 2020.

106   **United's MileagePlus was valued at $21.9 billion:** J. T. Genter, "How Airlines Make Billions from

166   Monetizing Frequent Flyer Programs."

106 **the stock market values those airlines at merely $5 to $10 billion:** J. T. Genter, "How Airlines Make Billions from Monetizing Frequent Flyer Programs."

106 **Airline points are a currency:** Perhaps the best account of this analogy is Wendover Productions, "How Airlines Quietly Became Banks," YouTube.

107 **treats ordinary credit card spending the same as miles flown for purposes of accruing points:** Joann Muller, "Why Airlines Are Going Overboard to Win Your Loyalty."

107 **airlines are now basically banks that just happen, incidentally, to operate airlines:** Wendover Productions, "How Airlines Quietly Became Banks"; J. T. Genter, "How Airlines Make Billions from Monetizing Frequent Flyer Programs."

107 **small cities that rely on concentrated hubs pay even more:** Andrew R. Goetz and Christopher J. Sutton, "The Geography of Deregulation in the U.S. Airline Industry," 238, 250–56.

108 **Great Lakes Airlines offered a once-weekly turboprop service to Denver:** Chrissy Suttles, "Cheyenne Secures Commercial Air Service with American Airlines," *Wyoming Tribune Eagle*, August 7, 2018.

108 **That same year the airline reported a net profit of $1.4 billion:** "American Airlines Group Reports Fourth-Quarter and Full-Year 2018 Profit," American Airlines Newsroom, January 24, 2019.

108 **local leaders were able to entice United to offer one flight a day to Denver:** Dave Lerner, "Commercial Airline Service Returns to Cheyenne," *Cheyenne Post*, October 20, 2020.

108 **Cheyenne is not a participant in the Essential Air Services program:** In Wyoming, only Cody and Laramie are eligible EAS cities. See Department of Transportation, Eligible Essential Air Service (EAS) Communities (excluding Alaska and Hawaii) as of December 2021, https://www .transportation.gov/sites/dot.gov /files/2022-01/Current%20list %20of%20EAS-Eligible%20 communities%20excl%20AK%20 %20HI_Dec2021_0.pdf.

108 **under constant attack from members of Congress who have described it as wasteful spending:** Cong. Res. Serv., Essential Air Service 8–12, December 19, 2018. Most notably, former senator and presidential candidate John McCain (R-AZ). See Matt Sepic, "Bill Would End Federal Subsidies in 3 Rural

Minn. Airports," MPR News, February 17, 2011; "CCAGW Supports McCain Amendment Ending Essential Air Service," Council for Citizens Against Government Waste, press release, February 14, 2011.

109   increase in service-sector employment in an airport's metro area: Jan K. Brueckner, "Airline Traffic and Urban Economic Development," *Urb. Stud.* 40 (2003), 1455.

109   hub cities benefit disproportionally from the industry's growth: Andrew R. Goetz and Christopher J. Sutton, "The Geography of Deregulation in the U.S. Airline Industry," (1997), 238, 250–56.

109–110   with declines in flights in the west Tennessee city, it moved to St. Louis: Philip Longman and Lina Khan, "Terminal Sickness," *Washington Monthly*, March 1, 2012.

110   "economic power that either constitutes or closely resembles monopoly power": Roy Goldberg, "Airline Challenges to Airport Abuses of Economic Power," *J. Air L. & Com.* 72 (2007), 351.

110   it opens up access to every destination the hub reaches: Alfred E. Kahn, "The Competitive Consequence of Hub Dominance: A Case Study," *Rev. Ind. Org.* 8 (1993), 381.

110   "Hub-spoke network[s] make it difficult for regional carriers to survive": Ken Hendricks, Michele Piccione, and Guofu Tan, "Entry and Exit in Hub-Spoke Networks," *Rand J. Econ* 28 (1997), 291.

111   "Airports cannot readily increase the supply of landing slots": *Air Transp. Ass'n of Am. v. U.S. Dept. of Transp.*, 613 F.3d 206 (D.C. Cir. 2010)

111   may also have considerable power to prevent new entrants: See Andrew Goetz, "Deregulation, Competition, and Antitrust Implications in the US Airline Industry," *J. Transport Geography*, 10 (2002), 1; Michael E. Levine, "Airline Competition in Deregulated Markets."

111   Airport and Airway Improvement Act of 1982: currently codified at 49 U.S.C. 47107.

111   Airlines that are being treated unfairly are not allowed to bring lawsuits themselves: *Compare New York Airlines, Inc. v. Dukes County*, 623 F.Supp. 1435 (D.Mass., 1985) with *Northwest Airlines, Inc. v. County of Kent*, 955 F.2d 1054 (6th Cir., 1992).

111   allow airlines to reject any new construction project at the airport: FAA/OST Task Force Study, Airport Business Practices and Their Impact on Airline

168   Competition ix–x, Federal Aviation Administration, October 1999.

112   **to ensure fair and reasonable prices for access to airports:** 114 Stat. 89. For an early account of lease restrictions, see "The Antitrust Implications of Airport Lease Restrictions," Notes, *Harv. L. Rev.* 104 (1990), 548.

112   **a tiny airfield with a two-story building terminal that opened in 2008:** Mike Tierney, "Tiny Airport Fights for Sliver of Atlanta Market," *New York Times,* December 22, 2014.

113   **they are surprisingly vulnerable when it comes to climate change and cyberattacks:** For a general discussion of the problems of resilience and the need to address them, see Ganesh Sitaraman, "A Grand Strategy of Resilience," *Foreign Affairs,* September/October 2020.

113   **The day before, it canceled 543 flights, more than 10 percent of its total:** Pete Muntean and Ramishah Maruf, "American Airlines Cancels More Than 600 Flights on Sunday," CNN, October 31, 2021.

113   **ninety-seven of the top hundred airports in the world failed a basic cybersecurity evaluation:** Davey Winder, "Airport Security Concern as 97% of World's Top 100 Fail Cybersecurity Test," *Forbes,* February 7, 2020.

113   **commentators rushed to blame Southwest's route structure:** Paul Krugman, "Learning from the Southwest Airlines Fiasco," *New York Times,* December 29, 2022.

114   **The subsequent lawsuits took years:** Timothy M. Ravich, *Introduction to Aviation Law* (2020), 376–77.

115   **began charging for each component separately:** Rachel Y. Tang, "Airline Passenger Rights: The Federal Role in Aviation Consumer Protection," Cong. Res. Serv., August 17, 2016.

115   **required creation of a toll-free consumer hotline, among other things:** H.R. 3051, Airline Passenger Protection Act of 1987, 100th Cong., https://www .congress.gov/bill/100th-congress /house-bill/3051?s=1&r=1.

116   **everything from deceptive advertising to unfair practices in a frequent flyer program:** *Morales v. Trans World Airlines, Inc.,* 504 U.S. 374 (1992); *American Airlines Inc. v. Wolens,* 513 U.S. 219 (1995); *Northwest, Inc. v. Ginsburg,* 572 U.S. 273 (2014).

116   **ensure "safe and adequate service":** 49 USC 41702.

116   **and they have continued to fail:** See, e.g., Sen. Ron Wyden, "Wyden Introduces Bill of Rights for Airline Passengers," press

release, August 2, 2019, https://
www.wyden.senate.gov/news/press
-releases/wyden-introduces-bill
-of-rights-for-airline-passengers-.

**116   diffuse majorities have a
more difficult time than
concentrated interest groups:**
Bruce A. Ackerman, "Beyond
Caroline Products," *Harv. L. Rev.* 98
(1985), 713.

**116–117   restricting its own
authority to regulate "unfair or
deceptive practices":** Defining
Unfair or Deceptive Practices, 85 FR
78707 (January 6, 2021) (to be
codified at 14 C.F.R. pt. 399).

**117   complaining that the
Obama-era regulations were too
stringent:** Ian Duncan, "Consumer
Groups Say New Trump
Administration Rules for Airlines
Will Hurt Efforts to Stop 'Deceptive
Practices,'" *Washington Post*,
November 30, 2020.

**117   "exciting, yet chaotic,
destined to result in a weak,
maimed industry":** Gary Kennedy
with Terry Maxon, *Twelve Years of
Turbulence: The Inside Story of
American Airlines' Battle for Survival*
(2018).

CHAPTER FIVE

**122   restrictions on foreign
carriers operating within US
territory:** For a discussion of these
and other restrictions, see Ganesh
Sitaraman, "The Regulation of

Foreign Platforms," *Stanford Law
Review* 74 (May 2022).

**125   is to widen geographic
inequality between regions:**
Ganesh Sitaraman, Morgan Ricks,
and Christopher Serkin,
"Regulation and the Geography of
Inequality," *Duke L.J.* 70 (2021),
1763.

**126   a popular writer will suggest
nationalizing the airlines:** See,
e.g., Jeff Macke, "American Airlines
Files for Bankruptcy: Is
Nationalization Next?" *Yahoo!
Finance*, November 29, 2011; "Time
to Nationalize the Airline
Industry?" *The Week*, January 11,
2015.

**126   spent their profits on stock
buybacks, before asking for
government support:** Alexander
Sammon, "It's Time to Nationalize
the Airlines," *American Prospect*,
March 18, 2020.

**127   would optimize choices
across air, rail, and transit, in
order to minimize carbon
emissions:** Paris Marx,
"Nationalize the Airlines," *Jacobin*,
March 25, 2020.

**127   until legislative constraints
were placed on it, the US Postal
Service:** See, e.g., Richard B.
Kielbowicz, "Postal Enterprise: Post
Office Innovations with
Congressional Constraints,
1789–1970," May 30, 2000, https://
www.prc.gov/sites/default/files

170   /papers/enterprise.pdf; see also
Devin Leonard, "The Post Office
Almost Delivered Your First
E-Mail," Bloomberg, May 16, 2016.

129   **create a public option for air
travel:** Ganesh Sitaraman and Anne
Alstott, *The Public Option* (2019);
Ganesh Sitaraman and Anne
Alstott eds., *Politics, Policy, and
Public Options* (2021).

129   **competition between public
and private can spur competition
in both directions:** E. S. Savas, "An
Empirical Study of Competition in
Municipal Service Delivery," *Pub.
Admin. Rev.* 37 (1977), 717; E. S.
Savas, "Intracity Competition
Between Public and Private Service
Delivery," *Pub. Admin Rev.* 41 (1981),
46. One difference between
municipal refuse collection and
nationwide air service is that a
contract for the former can be
replaced after a term of years more
easily than the latter.

129–130   **serving identical
routes, on (roughly) identical
schedules:** John Quiggin,
"Evaluating Airline Deregulation
in Australia," *Australian Econ. Rev.*
30 (1997), 45.

130   **both public and private
airlines were financially viable:**
David G. Davies, "The Efficiency of
Public Versus Private Firms, the
Case of Australia's Two Airlines," *J.
L. & Econ.* (1971), 149.

130   **concluded that the
Australian market is a natural
duopoly:** John Quiggin, "Evaluating
Airline Deregulation in Australia,"
45, 46.

131   **bogs the airlines (and
regulators) down in complicated
rules that are hard to implement
effectively:** Steven M. Teles,
"Kludgeocracy: The American Way
of Policy," *New America*, December
10, 2012.

137   **horizontal shareholding is
actionable today under the
Clayton Act:** Einer Elhauge,
"Horizontal Shareholding."

137   **"an unfair method of
competition in air
transportation":** 49 U.S.C.
§41712(a). See Note, Jonathan
Edelman, "Reviving Antitrust
Enforcement in the Airline
Industry," *Mich. L. Rev.* 120 (2021),
125.

CONCLUSION

139   **economic policy defined by
deregulation, trade liberalization,
privatization, and fiscal austerity:**
Gary Gerstle, *The Rise and Fall of the
Neoliberal Order* (2022).

139   **The financial crisis
galvanized opposition to
deregulatory efforts in that
sector:** See, e.g., Tim Wu, *The Curse
of Bigness* (2018).

140   **setting the stage for economywide deregulation:** See Thomas K. McCraw, *Prophets of Regulation*.

140   **Some of the Chicago School's foundational research has since been debunked:** See George L. Priest, "The Origins of Utility Regulation and the 'Theories of Regulation' Debate," 36 *J. L. & Econ.* 289 (1993).

141   **four of the seven have between an 83 and 90 percent**

market share: Matthew Jinoo Buck, "How America's Supply Chains Got Railroaded," *American Prospect*, February 4, 2022.

143   **the most prominent academic article in the field of "regulated industries" during the last quarter century:** Joseph D. Kearney and Thomas W. Merrill, "The Great Transformation of Regulated Industries Law," 98 *Colum. L. Rev.* 1323 (1998).